COMPACT *Research*

Toxic Waste

Stuart A. Kallen

Energy and the Environment

ReferencePoint
Press®

San Diego, CA

© 2011 ReferencePoint Press, Inc.

For more information, contact:
ReferencePoint Press, Inc.
PO Box 27779
San Diego, CA 92198
www.ReferencePointPress.com

Picture credits:
Cover: Dreamstime and iStockphoto.com
Maury Aaseng: 32–34, 47–49, 62–65, 77–79
AP Images: 17
Science Photo Library: 10

LIBRARY OF CONGRESS CATALOGING-IN-PUBLICATION DATA

Kallen, Stuart A., 1955–
   Toxic waste / by Stuart A. Kallen.
     p. cm. — (Compact research series)
   Includes bibliographical references and index.
   ISBN-13: 978-1-60152-124-8 (hardback)
   ISBN-10: 1-60152-124-3 (hardback)
   1. Hazardous wastes—Juvenile literature. I. Title.
   TD1030.5.K35   2011
   363.72'87—dc22

                                                        2009052242

Contents

Foreword

As modern civilization continues to evolve, its ability to create, store, distribute, and access information expands exponentially. The explosion of information from all media continues to increase at a phenomenal rate. By 2020 some experts predict the worldwide information base will double every 73 days. While access to diverse sources of information and perspectives is paramount to any democratic society, information alone cannot help people gain knowledge and understanding. Information must be organized and presented clearly and succinctly in order to be understood. The challenge in the digital age becomes not the creation of information, but how best to sort, organize, enhance, and present information.

ReferencePoint Press developed the *Compact Research* series with this challenge of the information age in mind. More than any other subject area today, researching current issues can yield vast, diverse, and unqualified information that can be intimidating and overwhelming for even the most advanced and motivated researcher. The *Compact Research* series offers a compact, relevant, intelligent, and conveniently organized collection of information covering a variety of current topics ranging from illegal immigration and deforestation to diseases such as anorexia and meningitis.

The series focuses on three types of information: objective single-author narratives, opinion-based primary source quotations, and facts and statistics. The clearly written objective narratives provide context and reliable background information. Primary source quotes are carefully selected and cited, exposing the reader to differing points of view. And facts and statistics sections aid the reader in evaluating perspectives. Presenting these key types of information creates a richer, more balanced learning experience.

For better understanding and convenience, the series enhances information by organizing it into narrower topics and adding design features that make it easy for a reader to identify desired content. For example, in *Compact Research: Illegal Immigration*, a chapter covering the economic impact of illegal immigration has an objective narrative explaining the various ways the economy is impacted, a balanced section of numerous primary source quotes on the topic, followed by facts and full-color illustrations to encourage evaluation of contrasting perspectives.

The ancient Roman philosopher Lucius Annaeus Seneca wrote, "It is quality rather than quantity that matters." More than just a collection of content, the *Compact Research* series is simply committed to creating, finding, organizing, and presenting the most relevant and appropriate amount of information on a current topic in a user-friendly style that invites, intrigues, and fosters understanding.

Toxic Waste at a Glance

Threat to People and the Environment

Toxic waste poses a substantial threat to human health and the environment when improperly managed.

Hazardous to Handle

Toxic waste is difficult to handle because it may be ignitable, corrosive, explosive, or poisonous.

Hundreds of Chemicals

The U.S. Environmental Protection Agency (EPA) classifies approximately 650 chemicals as toxic waste; many of these chemicals are produced in the manufacture of everyday products.

Lasting Effects

Some toxic wastes, such as dioxins and PCBs, are the most poisonous substances on Earth and are virtually indestructible in the environment.

Lagging Cleanup Efforts

Since the Superfund was created in 1980, over 1,080 U.S. hazardous waste sites have been cleaned up; more than 1,250 contaminated sites remain.

Expensive to Regulate

Between 2000 and 2009, the number of facilities producing hazardous waste in the United States more than doubled while the EPA budget for regulators remained the same.

Living Near Toxic Waste Sites

Superfund toxic waste sites can be found in nearly every state in the country; 1 out of every 4 Americans lives within 4 miles (6.4km) of a Superfund site.

Americans and Their Electronic Devices

E-waste is a major environmental concern because, every day, Americans throw out about 130,000 computers, 426,000 cell phones, and countless other electronic gadgets containing toxic chemicals.

E-Waste Recycling in the Developing World

Hazardous e-waste recycling practices threaten poor populations in China, India, and other parts of the developing world.

Overview

Overview

66Mismanagement of hazardous wastes, particularly improper disposal and accidental releases, can cause numerous threats to the public health and environment.99

—Milo Myers, director of environmental health, city of Albuquerque, New Mexico.

66[We] can have a vital, innovative, competitive chemicals industry with less—or even no—hazardous waste.99

—Rich Engler, program manager for EPA's Green Chemistry Program.

Every April Dow Chemical sponsors a fishing tournament in Midland, Michigan, in the shadow of its 1,900-acre (760ha) headquarters on the Tittabawassee River. The river is stocked with walleye, and the angler who catches the biggest fish wins $1,000. The prizewinner cannot eat the fish, however. Signs along the riverbank warn that fish in the Tittabawassee are contaminated with high levels of cancer-causing dioxins.

Dioxins are some of the most toxic chemicals on Earth. They are by-products of many manufacturing processes, including the making of paper and pesticides. When chlorine is used to bleach paper, for instance, the process produces dioxins. Dioxins are also found in the ashes of industrial waste when it is burned by garbage incinerators. In addition, dioxin pollution is associated with the production of polyvinyl chloride (PVC) plastic. This type of plastic is used in thousands of products from pool toys to construction materials such as pipes and electric wires.

Dow is one of the world's largest chemical manufacturers. It makes thousands of chemicals used in the production of plastics, paper, pesticides, and more. Many of those chemicals produce dioxin-laced waste products. Over the company's 100-plus years in business, the disposal, incineration, and emissions of dioxins have contaminated 50 miles (80.4km) of the Tittabawassee and Saginaw rivers in Midland and Saginaw Bay in Lake Huron.

What Is Toxic Waste?

Dioxin is just one of about 650 chemicals the U.S. Environmental Protection Agency (EPA) classifies as toxic, or hazardous, waste. This discarded material is an international concern. Toxic waste is produced by wealthy industrialized countries including the United States, Canada, the United Kingdom, Germany, France, and Japan. Hazardous waste is also a problem in developing nations such as China and India.

Wherever it is produced, toxic waste comes in many forms and travels through the environment in a myriad of ways. Toxins from incinerator smokestacks rise into the air as gases or solids, called particulates, and settle onto the land. Toxic waste is also poured into streams, rivers, lakes, and oceans from pipes, or it seeps into underground water reservoirs, called aquifers, after it is buried underground.

Producers in the steel and petroleum industries began dumping toxic waste in the environment in the nineteenth century. But the amount and toxicity of the waste greatly increased in the postwar industrial boom that began in the late 1940s. However, companies that dumped deadly chemicals on land or discharged them into the air and water did so legally. That changed in 1980 when Congress enacted the Comprehensive Environmental Response, Compensation and Liability Act (CERCLA). This law, commonly referred to as the Superfund, was enacted to prevent discharges of toxic waste. CERCLA also empowers the EPA to clean up sites that have been contaminated by toxic waste. These are known as

> **Dioxin is so toxic that three pounds of the substance would kill everyone in New York City.**

A thick, black, toxic soup oozes from barrels of waste illegally dumped on unused industrial land in Great Britain. Improper disposal of toxic waste poses a substantial threat to human health and the environment.

Superfund sites. CERCLA defines toxic waste as a substance that has the potential to "cause, or significantly contribute to an increase in mortality or an increase in serious irreversible, or incapacitating reversible illness; or pose a substantial or potential hazard to human health or the environment when improperly treated, stored, transported, or disposed of, or otherwise managed."[1]

A waste product is considered hazardous if it is ignitable (can easily catch fire), corrosive (eats away at material), reactive (explodes), or toxic (poisonous). Ignitable waste creates fires at low temperatures, less than 140°F (60°C). Common ignitable substances include paint thinners, degreasers, and other industrial solvents. Waste that is corrosive can dissolve material, including steel. These chemicals are either strong acids or alkalies. Such waste includes lye, rust removers, sulfuric acid, hydrochloric acid, battery acid, and some cleaning fluids. Over time, corrosives destroy the containers in which they are stored. Reactive wastes are chemically unstable and react when heated, compressed, or mixed with water or other materials. Reactive wastes may create explosions or produce toxic gases. For example, lithium, which is used to make lithium-sulfur batteries for electric cars, will burst into flames if mixed with water. A final classification of hazardous waste concerns radioactive wastes created by hospital X-ray machines and nuclear power plants.

Health Dangers Posed by Toxic Waste

Toxic waste is dangerous to human health. Some toxins, such as the potent poison arsenic, will immediately cause violent stomach pains, delirium, and death. However, arsenic is a naturally occurring substance; as such, it is biodegradable. That means that over time it can be broken down in the environment by natural processes. But arsenic and other naturally occurring toxins are extremely hazardous when large quantities are released into the environment during mining or industrial processes.

Dioxins and many other toxic wastes are not biodegradable. They are virtually indestructible and will remain in the environment for centuries. Nonbiodegradable toxic waste can cause chronic health problems over long periods of exposure. Dioxins have been linked to cancer, birth defects, miscarriages, decreased fertility, reduced sperm counts, diabetes, learning disabilities, lung problems, skin disorders, and more. Dioxin is so toxic that three pounds of the substance would kill everyone in New York City.

One of the ways researchers categorize hazardous waste is by the health problems the chemicals create. For example, waste classified as carcinogenic causes cancer in humans and animals. Teratogenic waste causes birth defects such as mental retardation and cleft palates. One of the most common teratogenic wastes is called PCB (polychlorinated biphenyl), formerly used as insulating fluids in industrial electrical transformers. Mutagenic substances, such as the radioactive waste generated by nuclear power plants, causes mutations in the genes of fetuses.

Mining Produces Toxic Waste

Virtually every industrial sector of modern society produces toxic waste. Poisons are created when basic elements are mined. They are left behind when consumer goods are produced. And toxic waste is contained in garbage generated by households, construction, and industry.

The process known as hard rock mining produces about 30 percent of all toxic waste in the United States. When miners extract silver, gold, copper, and other industrial minerals from the earth, they also pollute the environment with poisons such as arsenic, cadmium, lead, and mercury. Even tiny amounts of these substances are harmful to humans and wildlife, and they can travel long distances in water.

Sulfur is another waste product exposed during hard rock mining, and it causes a problem called acid mine drainage. Sulfur-laden rock is commonly found around mining sites. When this rock is exposed to air and water, it forms sulfuric acid, which drains into rivers and streams, killing aquatic plants and animals. At the abandoned Iron Mountain Mine in California, acid mine drainage produces water that is 10,000 times more acidic than battery acid.

> " Lithium, which is used to make lithium-sulfur batteries for electric cars, will burst into flames if mixed with water. "

In 2008, according to the EPA's Toxics Release Inventory (TRI), hard rock mining produced 105 million pounds (47.6 million kg) of arsenic, 369 million pounds (167.4 million kg) of lead, and 4 million pounds 1.8 million kg) of mercury. These toxins contaminate 40 percent of all watersheds in the western United States. Coal mining is similarly destructive. Thousands of miles of watersheds have been permanently polluted with sulfuric acid that originated in coal waste.

Manufacturing and Toxic Waste

Manufacturing industries are responsible for more than half of all toxic waste produced in the United States. Some of the most dangerous Superfund sites were created by chemical companies such as Dow, Monsanto, and Dupont. These companies' products, used by consumers worldwide, include plastics, pesticides, herbicides, and cleaning agents. However, their production leaves massive amounts of toxic by-products behind. For example, the production of chlorine bleach, cleanser, toilet bowl cleaner, and similar products creates waste laden with mercury and asbestos.

Chemical plants that produce carbon dioxide gas for soda and other drinks also create chromium, copper, and other heavy metal waste. Pigment production for paint results in corrosive sludge contaminated with cadmium, lead, and other metals. And chemical plants leave behind toxic waste from cleaning processes. For example, the air-pollution-control devices that prevent toxic chemicals from leaving factory smokestacks are laden with toxic elements that must be properly handled.

> " Plants that produce carbon dioxide gas for soda and other drinks also create chromium, copper, and other heavy metal waste. "

Because of the toxic waste they produce, chemical plants often generate controversy. For example, Dupont's DeLisle plant on the Mississippi Gulf Coast makes a chemical called super-white titanium dioxide. This substance is used in virtually all toothpaste, a product used by billions of people every day. However, production of this widely used substance at Dupont's DeLisle plant results in the creation of more than 12 million pounds (5.5 million kg) of dioxins, chromium, and nickel waste annually.

Plastic Production Creates Toxic Waste

The petroleum industry is also responsible for many types of toxic waste. It is created when gasoline, motor oil, brake fluid, antifreeze, and other fluids for automobiles are made. And petroleum products are combined with chlorine to make plastic, generating some of the most toxic substances on Earth.

Common plastics like polyethylene, polyvinyl chloride (PVC), polystyrene, and polyurethane are used to make millions of products, from toys to automobiles. Worldwide, over 100 million tons (90.7 million metric tons) of plastic is produced every year. One of the most common types of plastic, polyethylene terephthalate, or PET, is used to make water bottles. Americans throw away about 2.5 million PET water bottles every hour, or 60 million a day. The production of PET bottles generates highly toxic nickel, ethyl oxide, and benzene. And the production of a single 16-ounce PET bottle (480ml) generates 100 times more toxic waste than a glass bottle of the same size.

Toxic Waste Disposal in Other Countries

Proper management of hazardous waste requires treatment and disposal facilities such as waste incinerators and landfills. But in developing nations there are few environmental laws governing where and how such facilities are built. For example, in Dakar, Senegal, a hazardous waste landfill was built very close to the aquifer that supplies drinking water to the city's 2.5 million residents.

Dishonest government officials are part of the hazardous waste problem in many developing countries. According to Olurominiyi Ibitayo, a professor of urban environmental planning, a "high level of corruption is prevalent in . . . African countries hence government officials, both elected and appointed, can easily be bribed to . . . [overlook] unregulated dumping of toxic waste.[2]

By contrast, the European Union (EU) strictly regulates the 98 million tons (88.9 million metric tons) of hazardous waste produced annually by its 27 member nations. An extremely complex law called Registration, Evaluation, Authorisation and Restriction of Chemicals (REACH), was enacted in 2007 to control the production and disposal of toxic chemicals.

Disposal Practices in the United States

In the United States 256 million tons (232.2 million metric tons) of toxic waste is produced every year. The EPA controls toxic waste from what the agency calls "cradle-to-grave."[3] This means the government has the authority to regulate the entire life cycle of a toxic substance from production to use to disposal. There are several EPA-approved methods for disposing of hazardous waste. The most common method is used by the largest chemical and petroleum manufacturers. These companies pump toxins into underground sites in a process called deep well injection, or DWI. A typical DWI system consists of pipes that descend several thousand feet into the ground. Waste pumped into the pipes travels down to natural caves and permeable rock where it remains. One prominent example is the Dupont DeLisle plant which has the third largest DWI system in the country.

In 2008 Dupont pumped over 13 million tons (11.8 million metric tons) of waste into the earth through the DWI system. However, DWI systems are problematic. They often leak toxic substances into underground water reservoirs called aquifers. Residents who live around the DeLisle plant report that their tap water smells and that the water in their toilets is black and greasy. Some have reported getting painful blisters on their skin after showering. The situation has prompted hundreds of local residents to sue Dupont. In one lawsuit a local fisherman named Glen Ray Strong, who has a rare type of cancer called multiple myeloma, said Dupont "fraudulently concealed and intentionally misrepresented information about their toxic chemicals . . . with the full knowledge that their toxic [waste] could cause severe injury and even death."[4]

> " The production of a single 16-ounce (480ml) PET [plastic] bottle generates 100 times more toxic waste than a glass bottle of the same size. "

Toxic waste is also disposed of in special landfills that operate with government permits. There are various types of hazardous waste landfills, including traditional garbage dump facilities. Hazardous waste landfills are designed with clay liners and plastic barriers that are intended to prevent waste from seeping into the ground. Despite efforts to protect groundwater, however, many toxic landfills leak pollutants into aquifers where they are extremely difficult and costly to remove.

Incineration is considered the most effective way to neutralize toxic waste. The waste is burned at a very high heat, around 2,000°F (1,093°C), and converted into carbon dioxide, water, and nontoxic by-products. However, incinerating wastes causes mercury and dioxin air pollution. And the ash left after incineration remains contaminated and must be disposed of at landfills.

How Serious a Problem Is Toxic Waste?

Toxic waste not only comes from the mining, chemical, and petroleum industries, but is produced by small businesses. These include dry cleaners, photo processors, and car repair shops, which are not monitored by the EPA. Consumers also produce toxic waste when they dispose of household products such as used motor oil, pesticides, paints, and burned-out fluorescent light bulbs, which contain mercury.

Because of past disposal practices, which were unregulated, the EPA estimates that 36,000 seriously contaminated waste sites are in the United States. An additional 600,000 contaminated sites are known as brownfields. These are abandoned industrial properties that hold deserted factories, commercial buildings, or other operations that created toxic waste. Small brownfields also may be found in many residential neighborhoods. For example, abandoned filling stations with leaking underground gas tanks are classified as toxic brownfields. While not as contaminated as Superfund sites, the sheer number of brownfields is a cause for concern among environmentalists.

> " The United Nations estimates that 50 million tons (45.3 million metric tons) of e-waste is discarded worldwide every year. "

Are Toxic Waste Cleanup Efforts Working?

In 2008 more than 150 cities had successfully redeveloped 1,578 brownfield sites, returning more than 10,000 acres to productive economic use. These actions resulted in the creation of more than 191,000 jobs and generated $408 million in revenue.

Superfund sites are registered on what the EPA calls the National Priorities List (NPL). Unlike brownfields, these sites are not as easily returned to productive use. And about 22 new sites are added to the NPL every year. About 1,080 have been cleaned up and taken off the list since 1982. And in 2009 nearly 1,300 contaminated NPL sites remained. Many of these toxic waste sites are in populous areas. EPA figures show that 1 in every 4 Americans lives within 4 miles (6.4km) of a Superfund site.

How Big a Threat Is Electronic Waste?

Electronic waste, or e-waste, is produced when people throw away unwanted consumer electronics, including computers, televisions, cell phones, printers, MP3 players, fax machines, and entertainment systems. This type of waste poses a new threat to human health and the environment.

The United Nations estimates that 50 million tons (45.3 million metric tons) of e-waste is discarded worldwide every year. Nations in Asia discard about 13.2 million tons (12 million metric tons) of e-waste annually, the European Union produces about 10 million tons (9.1 million metric tons), and the United States creates 3 million tons (2.7 million metric tons).

At a scrap yard near Shanghai, China, workers sort automotive electronics and other car parts for recycling. The recycling of electronic waste has become big business in the developing world despite serious health risks for workers and nearby residents.

The components in e-waste contain some of the most dangerous toxins on Earth. A cathode ray tube (CRT) used in an old-style computer monitor or television can contain 3 to 7 pounds (1.3 to 3.1kg) of lead, a nervous system toxin, or neurotoxin. More than 20 million old CRTs were disposed of in U.S. landfills in 2008.

> **Many companies are working to reduce their reliance on toxic substances.**

Other forms of e-waste are also dangerous. Circuit boards used in computers, cell phones, and other electronics contain a wide array of dangerous heavy metals, including copper, cadmium, zinc, chromium, silver, nickel, antimony, beryllium, and barium. And every day, Americans throw out about 130,000 computers, 426,000 cell phones, and countless other electronic gadgets. This is creating what the *Wall Street Journal* calls "the world's fastest growing and potentially most dangerous waste problem."[5]

What Is the Future of Toxic Waste?

During the recession of 2009, the administration of President Barack Obama directed $600 million toward speeding up long-term cleanup actions at Superfund sites. Meanwhile, scientists, corporations, and environmentalists continued to seek new ways to deal with toxic waste. Most future plans deal with implementing recycling programs for waste, reducing the creation of toxins, and finding new ways to clean up old waste sites.

Recycling is playing an increasingly important role in containing waste materials. Retailers such as Best Buy, Staples, and Office Depot are working to create safe, efficient recycling programs for consumers' old electronics. However, not all electronics can be recycled through large retailers. For example, Best Buy does not take old-style TVs with CRT screens larger than 32 inches.

The most efficient method for reducing hazardous pollution is to not create toxins. And many companies are working to reduce their reliance on toxic substances. To help this cause the EPA instituted the National Waste Minimization Program in 2002. According to the agency Web site, the program "supports efforts that promote a more sustainable society, reduces the amounts of waste generated, and lowers the toxicity and persistence of wastes that are generated."[6]

A notable example of toxic waste minimization concerns computer manufacturing. Companies such as Dell, Apple, and others are producing "greener" computers made with fewer toxic materials. Apple led the industry by producing mercury-free monitors in 2009. The company also removed all PVCs and highly toxic brominated flame retardants (BFRs) from their product line.

A March 2009 Gallup poll shows that 80 percent of Americans have significant worries about soil and water contaminated with toxic waste. Therefore, manufacturers that reduce and recycle hazardous materials not only save money but improve their public image. But it will require that consumers, corporations, and government agencies that work together to reduce the toxic legacy of modern society so future generations can live in a less toxic world.

How Serious a Problem Is Toxic Waste?

66Clearly a toxic nightmare prevails in hundreds of communities who face corporate assaults of hazardous [waste] in incredible amounts.99

—Eddie J. Girdner and Jack Smith, environmental journalists.

66EPA will strive to accelerate the pace of cleanup at the hundreds of contaminated sites across the country ... reducing threats to human health and the environment ... our communities and our people.99

—Lisa P. Jackson, administrator of the EPA.

Toxic waste is generated by consumers and small businesses in nearly every nation on Earth. But much of the toxic waste in the environment is created by huge multinational corporations that operate in dozens of countries. One of the world's largest chemical companies, BASF, is based in Germany; the corporation has 150 production sites in Europe, Asia, Australia, the Americas, and Africa. BASF plants produce a wide variety of chemicals, plastics, acids, dyes, ammonia, and other substances. In 2008 BASF production facilities worldwide created about 1.65 million tons (1.5 million metric tons) of toxic waste.

Competitors of BASF, such as Dow, Dupont, Eastman Chemical, Shell, Bayer, ExxonMobil, and Mitsubishi, also operate in many nations.

In the United States alone, 170 major chemical companies run more than 2,800 chemical production plants located on almost every continent. Nearly all of these plants generate toxic waste.

No matter how toxic waste is generated or where, it presents dangerous health problems for humans and animals and damages the environment. Many of the chemicals are unfamiliar to the average citizen, but some are well known. They have gained widespread notoriety for their persistence in the environment and their deadly effects on human and animal health.

Toxic Hydrocarbons

Hydrocarbons are toxic compounds made from hydrogen and carbon. They are usually derived from petroleum or a thick black liquid called coal tar. Hydrocarbons form the basis for many industrial chemicals and many types of toxic waste. One example is benzene, created in the production of drugs, dyes, plastics, nylon, and synthetic rubber. Benzene compounds are some of the most poisonous hydrocarbons. Benzene is carcinogenic, teratogenic, and combustible, and more than 100 Superfund sites in the United States are contaminated with benzene.

Another group of highly poisonous toxic waste products are called halogenated hydrocarbons. One of the deadliest forms of halogenated hydrocarbon is the chemical TCP (trichlorophenol), commonly used in the manufacture of weed killers, or herbicides. When TCP is created, it produces dioxin, the single most cancer-causing agent known to science.

Halogenated hydrocarbons referred to as PCBs are related to dioxins. The group of 36 related chemicals was banned in 1985 but remain a major problem. These chemicals, which cause cancer, birth defects, and other health problems, are found nearly everywhere, linger in the environment for centuries, and are nearly impossible to clean up.

Problems with Heavy Metals

Heavy metals are another major group of chemicals present in toxic waste. They are called heavy metals because they have an atomic weight at least five times that of water. They are natural components of Earth's crust and cannot be degraded or destroyed.

The electronics, automobile, and steel industries use more than 20 kinds of heavy metals. Circuit boards, which perform computing functions in thousands of electronic devices, use many types of heavy metals including gold, arsenic, barium, chromium, copper, lead, mercury, selenium, and silver.

Another major source of heavy metal pollution comes from household trash. Batteries used in everyday household items such as flashlights, video game controllers, clocks, and remote control devices are not supposed to be thrown away with other household garbage but often are. They contain lead, lithium, nickel, and cadmium and contribute from 50 to 70 percent of heavy metals in landfills.

Dumping Heavy Metals

Every business that works with heavy metals produces toxic waste. Companies are supposed to properly dispose of the waste under tightly regulated conditions. But often the toxic waste finds its way into the environment. And companies that dump the waste face few consequences. Between 2003 and 2008, a zinc smelter called Horsehead Corporation, located near Pittsburgh, Pennsylvania, illegally dumped heavy metal waste such as copper, lead, zinc, and selenium into the Ohio River more than 135 times.

> " The EPA is overwhelmed by the increasing number of companies that are generating toxic waste. "

When a company dumps this type of toxic waste it is violating the Clean Water Act, established in 1972 to protect the country's waterways from many types of pollution. Despite the law, fewer than 3 percent of such violations result in fines or other punishment. Commenting on the situation, Minnesota representative James L. Oberstar told the *New York Times*: "I don't think anyone realized how bad things have become. . . . The E.P.A. and states have completely dropped the ball. Without oversight and enforcement, companies will use our lakes and rivers as dumping grounds—and that's exactly what is . . . going on."[7]

Budget Cuts Affect Enforcement

Oberstar is concerned that the EPA is overwhelmed by the increasing number of companies that are generating toxic waste. Between 2000 and

2009, the number of facilities producing hazardous waste in the United States more than doubled while the EPA budget remained the same, when adjusted for inflation. As a result, the agency employed the same number of inspectors that it did in the 1990s, while their workloads doubled.

The EPA works with state regulators who provide enforcement of local and federal toxic waste regulations. However, the deep economic recession that began in 2008 resulted in massive budget cuts at state environmental agencies. For example, in 2009 the Pennsylvania Department of Environmental Protection (DEP) faced a budget cut of 27 percent, leaving only three inspectors to monitor toxic waste violations in the entire eastern half of the state, which includes Philadelphia and other large cities.

> " Between 2000 and 2009, the number of facilities producing hazardous waste in the United States more than doubled. "

Illegal Dumping

Even without budget cuts, environmental regulators find it difficult to monitor toxic waste dumped by powerful industries. This was the case in the Appalachian Mountains of West Virginia where coal companies illegally dumped toxic waste for more than a decade. West Virginia is the second largest producer of coal in the United States. Coal production has created a host of environmental problems.

Around 1999, people living in Prenter, about 17 miles (27km) from the state capital in Charleston, noticed their well water was sometimes gray and oily. Bathtubs and sinks were stained with reddish rings that could not be removed. The water was tested, and results showed the formerly clean wells were tainted with dangerous levels of lead, manganese, barium, and other metals.

The water problem was traced to nine nearby mining operations run by Peabody Energy, the largest coal company in the United States. In order to remove rock and other debris from the coal, it is ground into a fine powder and mixed with water. This produces a black liquid waste product called slurry or sludge that contains dozens of unwanted chemicals.

Peabody stored the slurry in huge ponds called sludge impoundments and also injected it into abandoned coal mines for storage underground. This is an approved method for disposing of toxic mining waste, but companies are required, at great expense, to remove hazardous chemicals from the slurry before storing it.

Overwhelmed Inspectors

Records show the coal company injected more than 1.9 billion gallons (7.2 billion L) of coal slurry into the ground near Prenter between 2004 and 2009, and millions of gallons were dumped into lagoons. And this was not unique. Over 350 coal mining companies and related facilities in West Virginia were shown to have illegally dumped manganese, aluminum, iron, and other heavy metals into the state's waterways without being warned by the DEP.

> Heavy metals negatively affect the nervous system and cause cardiovascular problems, such as high blood pressure and heart disease.

The water violations did gain the attention of Matthew Crum, an inspector who joined the DEP in 2001. However, after Crum shut down several mines for violating toxic waste laws he was fired. In the aftermath, the dumping of toxic waste continued unabated. After Crum's firing, dozens of DEP regulators quit their jobs and began working for the coal companies they formerly regulated. According to one anonymous DEP employee, "We are outmanned and overwhelmed, and that's exactly how industry wants us. It's been obvious for decades that we're not on top of things, and coal companies have earned billions relying on that."[8]

Effects of Toxic Waste on Human Health

The illegal dumping of toxic waste is blamed for many health problems in Prenter, where people depend on wells for drinking water. A study of a group of 100 affected people showed that 30 percent had to have their gall bladders removed and half had damaged tooth enamel and chronic stomach diseases. On one short stretch of highway near the mines, five people were diagnosed with brain tumors.

Peabody denied it was responsible for the illnesses in Prenter and issued a report saying water in its injection sites flowed away from nearby residences. However, Ben Stout, a biology professor who tested the water, stated, "I don't know what else could be polluting these wells. The chemicals coming out of people's taps are identical to the chemicals the coal companies are pumping into the ground."[9]

Like the citizens of Prenter, millions of people are exposed to heavy metals every year. Most heavy metals are fat soluble, which means they are stored in the body fat. Heavy metals also bioaccumulate, or build up in the body. After repeated exposures the accumulation results in health problems. Heavy metals negatively affect the nervous system and cause cardiovascular problems, such as high blood pressure and heart disease. Infants and young children are especially sensitive to even low levels of heavy metals, which may contribute to learning and behavioral problems and lowered IQ.

> " Dioxin levels in large fish . . . are 100,000 times that of the surrounding environment. "

Like heavy metals, PCBs and dioxins are fat soluble and bioaccumulate. People absorb these chemicals mainly by consuming food, especially fish, meat, and dairy products. Exposure has been linked to birth defects, inability to maintain pregnancy, decreased fertility, reduced sperm counts, diabetes, learning disabilities, immune system problems, lung problems, skin disorders, and lowered hormone levels.

The EPA calls dioxins and PCBs hydrophobic (water-fearing) and lipophilic (fat-loving)—to escape water, the chemicals seek the fat of fish. For this reason, dioxin levels in large fish such as walleye, which are popular with anglers, are 100,000 times that of the surrounding environment.

The fat-loving PCBs and dioxins also fall onto the land where the chemicals are absorbed by cows, pigs, and chickens. Studies show that an individual in the United States eating a typical American diet will receive 93 percent of his or her dioxins from beef, fish, pork, poultry, and dairy products.

The Debate over Toxic Waste and Health

Research shows that nearly everyone on Earth carries within their bodies PCBs, dioxins, heavy metals, and dozens of other chemicals considered toxic waste. In one study, blood samples were taken from top environmental officials from the United States and the European Union. Analysis showed that the officials had a total of 44 different hazardous chemicals in their bloodstreams. Every person tested carried benzene, cadmium, and cancer-causing dioxin by-products called furans. While none of the test subjects were sick, because of bioaccumulation, they might face serious health problems in the future.

However, there has been a long-running debate over the physical effects of toxic chemicals. The chemical industry argues that tiny amounts of toxins within the body do not affect human health. The industry also contends that chemical measuring techniques have improved so much in recent years that scientists are now able to measure exceedingly low concentrations of toxic waste chemicals in human tissue. As Elizabeth M. Whelan, president of the American Council on Science and Health, points out: "Concentrations measurable today are thousands-fold lower than we could detect even ten years ago. The mere ability to detect a chemical in the body is only an indication that exposure has occurred; it does not mean that there is any health hazard."[10]

> Measuring techniques have improved so much in recent years that scientists are now able to measure exceedingly low concentrations of toxic waste chemicals in human tissue.

Despite Whelan's assertion, research shows some chemicals may be more dangerous than previously believed, even at very low levels. Their toxic effects may be amplified by interacting with one another in ways that have not been studied. According to Linda S. Birnbaum, director of both the National Institute for Environmental Health Sciences (NIEHS) and the National Toxicology Program in Washington, D.C., "Some chemicals may act in an additive fashion. . . . When we look at one compound at a time, we may miss the boat."[11]

European regulators have adopted what is called the Precautionary Principle to deal with toxic waste. This principle says chemicals should be banned or strictly regulated even though uncertainties exist concerning their effect on the environment or health. Some believe the Precautionary Principle should be followed in the United States. However, manufacturers strongly resist such measures. As the debate rages, toxic waste will remain a complex problem as long as people continue to produce and consume the products of modern industrial society.

Primary Source Quotes*

How Serious a Problem Is Toxic Waste?

66 A child born in America today will grow up exposed to more chemicals [from toxic waste] than a child from any other generation in our history. . . . Our kids are getting steady infusions of industrial chemicals before we even give them solid food. 99

—Lisa P. Jackson, "Administrator Lisa P. Jackson, Remarks to the Commonwealth Club of San Francisco," EPA, September 9, 2009. http://yosemite.epa.gov.

Jackson is the administrator of the EPA.

66 [There] are so many chemicals that we know very, very little about . . . [and to] test all those chemicals adequately is probably not feasible. 99

—Linda S. Birnbaum, "Fooling with Nature," *Frontline*, 2008. www.pbs.org.

Birnbaum is director of the National Institute for Environmental Health Sciences (NIEHS) and the National Toxicology Program.

* Editor's Note: While the definition of a primary source can be narrowly or broadly defined, for the purposes of Compact Research, a primary source consists of: 1) results of original research presented by an organization or researcher; 2) eyewitness accounts of events, personal experience, or work experience; 3) first-person editorials offering pundits' opinions; 4) government officials presenting political plans and/or policies; 5) representatives of organizations presenting testimony or policy.

66 Toxic heavy metals in air, soil, and water are global problems that are a growing threat to humanity. 99

—Matthew M. Matlock, "Effectiveness of Commercial Heavy Metal Chelators with New Insights for the Future in Chelate Design," Techno Mine, 2009. http://technology.infomine.com.

Matlock is an environmental researcher in the Department of Chemistry, University of Kentucky.

66 [It] remains impossible to accurately calculate the severity of heavy metal toxicity across the population. 99

—Marek Doyle, "Mercury and Heavy Metal Toxicity: How Much of an Issue Are They?" *American Chronicle*, November 4, 2009. www.americanchronicle.com.

Doyle is a nutritional therapist.

66 No one ever purposefully ingested PCBs (at least not that I know of), yet we've all got them in us. And, more importantly, no one was ever asked if they minded being exposed to PCBs, DDT, dioxin or any other of these chemicals. 99

—Emily Monosson, "Chemicals We Love to Hate," The Neighborhood Toxicologist, April 27, 2009. http://theneighborhoodtoxicologist.blogspot.com.

Monosson is a toxicologist who specializes in data about pesticides, PCBs, and chemical mixtures.

66 Mercury contamination of fish and mammals is a global public health concern. Our study of fish tested in different locations around the world shows that widely accepted international exposure levels for mercury are exceeded, often by wide margins. 99

—Michael Bender, "Mercury in Fish a Global Health Concern: Warrants Immediate United Nations Action," Pollution Probe, February 10, 2009 www.pollutionprobe.org.

Bender is a researcher for the Zero Mercury Working Group.

66 The 'safe' level of mercury set by EPA is recognized to be the most stringent in the world and is known to be at least ten times higher than any actual levels of concern or harm established by other medical experts. 99

—Willie Soon, "More on Eating More Fish," *Frontiers of Freedom*, August 10, 2007. www.ff.org.

Soon is chief science researcher at the Center for Science and Public Policy.

66 Horrific violations of the Clean Water Act have reached a state of emergency in the coalfields. 99

—Jeff Biggers, "Where's the Love? Will Lisa Jackson and Nancy Sutley Ever Visit a Mountaintop Removal Site?" *Huffington Post*, November 17, 2009. www.huffingtonpost.com.

Biggers is author of *Reckoning at Eagle Creek: The Secret Legacy of Coal in the Heartland*.

66 Regulators inspect mining sites to ensure coal operators are adhering to environmental . . . standards. If those standards are violated, regulators will issue notices of violation that result in fines to the operator or (for serious infractions) even closure of the mine. 99

—Roger L. Nicholson, "Anti-mining Activists Neglect Facts in Rhetoric," *Huntington (WV) Herald-Dispatch*, December 7, 2008. www.wvcoal.com.

Nicholson is senior vice president of International Coal Group.

How Serious a Problem Is Toxic Waste?

- The 170 major chemical companies located in the United States produce toxic waste at **2,800 chemical facilities** worldwide.

- China creates approximately **11 million tons** (10 million metric tons) of toxic waste each year; India produces about **4.8 million tons** (4.4 million metric tons) annually.

- Internationally, the **mining industry** produces the most toxic waste followed by the chemical industry, the food and beverage industry, and the wood and paper industry.

- Every year American industries and small businesses produce about **1,700 pounds** (771kg) of toxic waste for every man, woman, and child in the United States.

- The EPA maintains a list called the **Toxics Release Inventory** that lists over 650 chemicals considered hazardous waste.

- As trace elements, some heavy metals such as copper, selenium, and zinc are essential to the metabolism of the human body. However, at high concentrations they are **poisonous**.

- **Fifty to 70 percent** of heavy metals in landfills come from batteries.

- Cheap **alkaline batteries** contain an extremely corrosive toxic chemical called potassium hydroxide that burns through linings designed to prevent toxic waste leakage.

Worldwide Toxic Waste Generation

Toxic waste is produced by both industrialized and developing nations but industrialized nations produce more of it. The United States produces an estimated 256 million tons (232.2 million metric tons) of toxic waste each year. The European Union, consisting of 27 countries, generates an estimated 98 million tons (88.9 million metric tons) of toxic waste annually. In the developing world, China generates an estimated annual output of 11 million tons (9.9 million metric tons), while India produces about 4.8 million tons (4.3 million metric tons) each year.

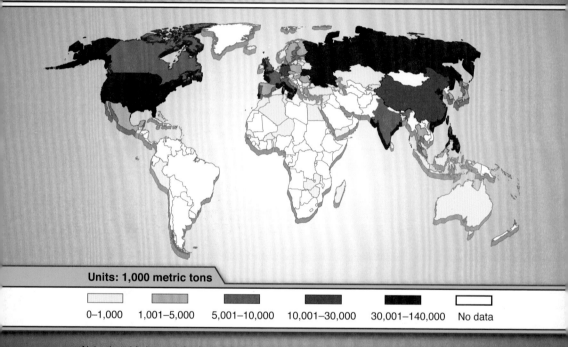

Units: 1,000 metric tons

0–1,000   1,001–5,000   5,001–10,000   10,001–30,000   30,001–140,000   No data

Note: 1 metric ton equals about 2,200 pounds

Source: United Nations Statistics Division, "Environmental Indicators: Hazardous Waste Generation," August 2009. www.unstats.un.org.

- While mercury was detected in the blood of only **2 percent** of all American women in 1999, it was found in **30 percent** of women by 2008.

- Research shows that an estimated **1 in 10 Americans** has been exposed to drinking water that contains chemicals linked to toxic waste.

Health and Environmental Effects

Exposure to toxic elements such as arsenic, chromium, and lead can have serious consequences for human health and the environment. For instance, in humans, arsenic can lead to cancer of the lungs, skin, and liver while exposure to lead can disrupt the nervous system and result in brain damage. In the environment, exposure to chromium can lead to cancer and respiratory problems in living organisms.

Metal/ Compound	Health Effects	Environmental Effects
Aluminum	Damage to central nervous system, dementia, memory loss, listlessness, severe trembling, lung damage, kidney problems, possible connection to Alzheimer's disease	Accumulation in plants can cause animals to become ill when they eat the plants, poisoning of animals that eat contaminated fish, amphibians, and insects; damage to tree roots
Arsenic	Irritation of stomach and intestines; decrease in production of red and white blood cells, skin changes; lung irritation, development of cancers, especially lung, skin, liver, and lymphatic; infertility and miscarriages; declined resistance to infections; heart disruptions; brain damage	Plants can absorb high amounts leading to high concentrations in the food supply; can poison animals and humans that eat contaminated fish
Beryllium	Berylliosis (dangerous and persistent lung disorder that can also damage the heart, 20 percent of patients will die); lung damage and pneumonia; allergic reactions; weakness, tiredness, and respiratory problems; increased risk of cancer	Some fruits and vegetables such as kidney beans and pears can contain significant levels of the metal, however most is excreted quickly enough that is does not do any damage, indication that there is a small cancer link
Chromium	Skin rashes; upset stomach and ulcers; respiratory problems; weakened immune system; kidney and liver damage; lung cancer; death	Toxic to organisms; can cause cancer in organisms; can cause respiratory problems, birth defects, infertility, and tumor formation in organisms; lower ability to fight disease and infection
Lead	Disruption of the biosynthesis of hemoglobin and anemia; rise in blood pressure; kidney damage in; miscarriages; disruption of nervous system; brain damage; decline in fertility of men through sperm damage; diminished learning abilities in children; Behavioral disruptions in children, such as aggression, impulsive behavior, and hyperactivity	Accumulates in the bodies of water and soil organisms; kills shellfish; phytoplankton can be damaged, which can lead to poisoning of many large sea animals; soil functions are disturbed; possible contamination of entire food chain
Manganese	Obesity; blood clotting; skin problems; lowered cholesterol levels; skeletal disorders; birth defects; changes in hair color; neurological symptoms	Can cause lung, liver, and vascular damage in animals; causes decline in blood pressure, brain damage, and distirubs fetal development in animals
Nickel	Sickness and dizziness after exposure to nickel gas; lung embolism; respiratory failure; birth defects; asthma and chronic bronchitis; allergic reactions such as skin rashes, mainly from jewelry; heart disorders	Can cause various types of cancer in animals that live close to refineries

Source: Lenntech, "Periodic Table: Elements," 2008. www.lenntech.com.

Understanding Landfills

Landfills provide a place for waste to be buried and isolated from surrounding soil, groundwater, and air. Some landfills only accept everyday waste, while others are designated specifically for toxic waste. Either way, the basic structure of the landfill is the same. In a municipal solid waste landfill a plastic liner rests on a layer of compacted clay to keep leachate from reaching groundwater below. Leachate is the mix of toxic substances that percolate out of waste. A collection pipe then routes those substances into a specifically designed pond. The arrows show the flow of leachate.

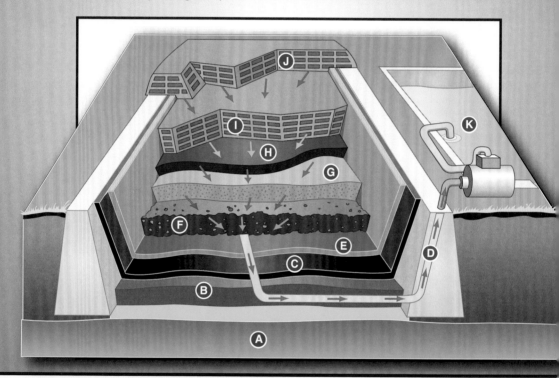

Ⓐ Ground Water		Ⓖ Drainage Layer
Ⓑ Compacted Clay		Ⓗ Soil Layer
Ⓒ Plastic Liner		Ⓘ Old Cells
Ⓓ Leachate Collection Pipe		Ⓙ New Cells
Ⓔ Geotextile Mat		Ⓚ Leachate Pond
Ⓕ Gravel		

Source: HowStuffWorks, "How Landfills Work," http://science.howstuffworks.com.

- Between 2000 and 2008, the number of **regulated polluters** in New York doubled to 19,000, but the number of EPA inspections remained about the same.

- According to one EPA study, federal regulators knew that between 2004 and 2009 at least **30 states** had major problems documenting which companies were violating the **Clean Water Act** with toxic waste.

- Selenium is a naturally occurring chemical element in coal that poses a significant environmental hazard, eliminating entire **communities of fish and birds** when released into waterways during the mining process.

- In 2008 the country's fourth-largest coal producer, Massey Energy Co., was fined **$20 million** for routinely polluting hundreds of streams and waterways in West Virginia and Kentucky with waste water and coal slurry.

Are Toxic Waste Cleanup Efforts Working?

❝The picture downstream of Hudson Falls was ghastly. Heavy metals, DDT and dioxins, tailings from pulp and paper mills, municipal sewage, and other contaminants presented a frightening scene.❞

—David Gargill, environmental journalist.

❝By dredging we're finally doing something to lower the PCB levels, forever.❞

— Kristen Skopeck, member of the EPA Hudson River PCB dredging project team.

Cleaning up toxic waste is one of the most costly and complex problems facing modern society. In some cases those responsible for creating the waste refuse to pay for expensive cleanup efforts. For example, in the Amazon rain forest of Ecuador, residents have been battling Texaco in court for years. They want the oil company to clean up 18 billion gallons of toxic waste created by decades of petroleum production. Researchers say the chemical brew, believed to be the worst case of oil-related contamination on Earth, has caused a cancer epidemic afflicting thousands of local residents. However, the company, now owned by Chevron, says responsibility for the cleanup lies with the Ecuadorian government.

In some cases cleaning up toxic waste is an overwhelming process that can take generations. In Great Britain, at the Sellafield nuclear power plant, scientists are trying to devise a way to clean up piles of old nuclear reactor parts and decaying fuel rods that emit deadly radiation. The manager of the plant has called the facility "the most hazardous industrial building in western Europe."[12] Cleanup is expected to cost more than $75 billion dollars and take 100 years to complete.

Another problem with cleaning up toxic waste is that certain toxins are so widespread that they cannot be contained. For example, on the frozen ice near the Arctic Circle, scientists have found polar bears suffering from birth defects caused by exposure to PCBs. These toxins were banned in the United States and many other countries in the 1970s, but they continue to travel through rivers and ocean currents as far as the Arctic where they persist in the environment.

Cleaning Up Superfund Sites

In September 2008 the EPA added six new hazardous waste sites to the more than 1,200 on the National Priorities List of Superfund sites. One of the sites is the 153-acre (62ha) Iron King Mine in Dewey-Humboldt, Arizona, which was abandoned in 1969. The site contains arsenic, lead, and other mining waste. Another site, Flash Cleaners, in Pompano Beach, Florida, was a dry cleaning facility from 1977 to 2001. Wastewater discharged into a septic tank resulted in surrounding soil and groundwater contaminated with highly toxic compounds used in the dry cleaning process. These chemicals are leaching into local drinking water. At the Old Esco Manufacturing site in Greenville, Texas, which was abandoned in 1991, PCBs from electrical transformer production were found in the soil to a depth of 15 feet. Thirty-five nearby properties were contaminated with the toxin.

> " **Capping is used when there is no threat that hazardous materials will drain into rivers or aquifers.** "

At each new Superfund site, the EPA follows a nine-step procedure that can take years to complete. The agency evaluates the threat, goes to court to place the site on the NPL, and conducts costly studies to determine the best methods for cleanup. Once these steps are completed, a report called a Record of Decision (ROD) is issued with specific information about the site, including history and descriptions of the cleanup. The next step, called remedial action, includes preparing for and performing the cleanup at the site. The final steps include tests to ensure the site is no longer a threat. After that the site is deleted from the NPL, and ways are found to return the former Superfund site to productive use.

Many Methods Are Used for Cleanup

One of the most common methods for cleaning up toxic waste is known as capping. Capping is used when there is no threat that hazardous materials will drain into rivers or aquifers. Such is the case the Old Esco site, where PCBs are present in the soil. Capping will be used to bury the toxins in a way that contains them within decay-resistant materials including synthetic fibers, heavy clays, and, sometimes, concrete.

At the Iron King Mine, where storage ponds are contaminated with heavy metals, the EPA uses a process called precipitation. During the precipitation process, water contaminated with heavy metals is treated with chemicals that cause the metal molecules to stick together and separate from the water. The clean water is returned to the ground while the metals are recycled or otherwise properly disposed of. However, precipitation can be extremely expensive in cases where many types of metals are found in the water. Each metal must be treated with a different chemical, and the processes may interfere with one another, making cleanup efforts difficult.

> When the Superfund was created the law stated that the 'polluter pays' for cleanup.

At the dry cleaning site in Florida, the EPA will undertake a process called excavation to dig up and remove the contaminated septic tank and surrounding soil. This relatively inexpensive process utilizes bulldozers, backhoes, front loaders, and dump trucks to remove hazardous waste and cart it away to an approved disposal site. However, excavation requires extreme care so that contamination does not spread to clean areas. Equipment used in the process must be thoroughly cleaned and decontaminated before it can be removed from the site.

In some cases contaminants that are removed from a Superfund site might be destroyed through incineration. This involves burning compounds such as dioxin and PCBs at high temperatures between 1,600°F and 2,500°F (871°C and 1371°C). The EPA strictly regulates conditions under which an incinerator can operate. During incineration small amounts of hazardous waste are released into the atmosphere through smokestacks. And while incineration is supposed to destroy 99 percent of all organic compounds, the EPA states that most incinerators are not operated at efficiency standards that ensure that rate of destruction. This means that the leftover ash and material removed from the incinerator are contaminated with toxic waste, which must be hauled, at great expense, to a hazardous waste landfill.

Superfund Success Stories

Once cleanup of a Superfund site is completed, that site receives a "construction completion" designation. As of December 2009, the construction completion designation was applied to 1,081 Superfund sites. This is an average of 40 such designations per year since the first cleanup was finished at Walcotte Chemical Company warehouses in Greenville, Mississippi, on December 30, 1982. This early success was easily accomplished because the Walcotte site was small, about one acre (0.4ha), and the toxic waste was stored in 225 steel drums. Once the drums were hauled away to a regulated landfill for safe disposal, the site was considered construction complete.

Most Superfund sites present more complications than the one in Greenville. For example, the 1,081st site on the completion list, finished November 25, 2009, was first added to the NPL in 1984. The 88-acre (35.6ha) Moss-American facility in Milwaukee County, Wisconsin, treated railroad ties with creosote, or naphthalene, a hy-

> " In 1998 the EPA recovered about $320 million from toxic waste polluters, but by 2006 that number had dropped to $60 million. "

drocarbon that causes cancer, skin rashes, and problems with the eyes, kidneys, and liver. Cleanup, which began in 1990, cost over $40 million and required several extremely complicated steps, including rerouting the nearby Little Menomonee River so that 26,000 tons (23,587 metric tons) of contaminated sediment could be dredged from the river bottom. And even after 25 years, the EPA notes that "human exposure to dangerous substances or migration of contaminated groundwater off the site are not under control."[13] This is typical at many sites where work has been completed and the last remnants of toxic waste left behind are too expensive to remove.

Top Polluters

The EPA cannot thoroughly clean many sites because of the way the agency pays for site cleanup, a process called mitigation. When the Superfund was created the law stated that the "polluter pays" for cleanup. This required companies, organizations, or individuals that contaminated a site to fund mitigation efforts. However, the cost of cleanup was so high that many polluters, called "potentially responsible parties" (PRPs), declared bankruptcy to avoid paying for remediation.

Many large corporations labeled PRPs fight the EPA in court so that they do not have to pay for mitigation. As a result, the amount of money the EPA collected from PRPs has declined sharply over the years. In 1998 the EPA recovered about $320 million from toxic waste polluters, but by 2006 that number had dropped to $60 million, the cost of cleaning up a medium-sized Superfund site.

> **Toxic waste in the river flows past New York City and into the Atlantic Ocean, making the Hudson one of the highest-profile Superfund cleanup efforts in the nation.**

At many Superfund sites, the PRP is the federal government itself. By 2009 about 20 percent of all Superfund sites were created by the Department of Defense (DOD) at military bases and weapons-testing sites. The DOD sites are among the most hazardous areas in the country, polluted with spent ammunition, chemical weapons, petrochemicals, rocket fuel, and radiological and biological materials that were dumped with little regulation or oversight for decades. Many of these sites will cost billions of dollars to clean up, and some mitigation efforts are expected to last up to 40 years.

After the federal government, some of the largest companies in the world are designated top PRPs. According to a 2007 EPA report, Honeywell International Inc., producer of weapons, computers, electronics, and other products, was the leader on the Top PRP list, linked to 128 Superfund sites. General Electric (GE), producer of appliances, electronic hardware, and military equipment was responsible for 116 sites. The world's largest oil company, Chevron Corporation, was associated with 122 sites. Other major companies include computer maker IBM (28 sites), electronics and metals producer Tyco International Ltd. (19 sites), and defense contractor Lockheed Martin Corp. (19 sites).

> " The story of GE, PCBs, and the EPA shows how difficult it is to clean up toxic waste when powerful forces in business and government oppose one another. "

The Hudson River and PCBs

In 2009 the EPA began working with GE to clean up a highly polluted Superfund site where PCBs were dumped in the Hudson River for decades. The toxic waste in the river flows past New York City and into the Atlantic Ocean, making the Hudson one of the highest-profile Superfund cleanup efforts in the nation. The EPA calls the Hudson cleanup a major success story. But the effort has been a bitter, decades-long battle between environmentalists, General Electric, GE workers, politicians, and the EPA. And critical issues concerning the effectiveness of the cleanup effort remain unresolved.

General Electric is the tenth most profitable corporation in the world. The company built its reputation in the early 1900s, providing electricity to millions of Americans. To deliver that power, GE built heavy-duty electrical equipment at its Industrial and Power Capacitor Division in two factories about 1 mile (0.6km) apart on the Upper Hudson River. One factory was in Hudson Falls, the other in Fort Edward, New York.

GE's electrical equipment utilized a liquid insulator called Pyranol, the company's commercial name for a synthetic oil composed of PCBs. Although GE stopped producing Pyranol in 1977, environmental journalist David Gargill writes that "chemical anthropologists will still be finding it thousands of years from now, assuming we're still around."[14] The EPA estimates that GE discharged 1.3 million pounds (0.6 million kg) of PCBs into the Hudson while another 1.6 million pounds (0.7 million kg) were found in an underground reservoir located under a parking lot at the Fort Edward facility.

In the early 1980s the EPA discovered that the river bottom sediment in the Hudson contained dangerously high levels of PCBs. However, when the agency required General Electric to pay for mitigation, GE initiated a costly legal battle against the EPA. Between 1990 and 2002, the company spent more than $122 million to fight the agency in court.

Toxic Waste Remains

After 12 years, the EPA won the court cases. In February 2002 the agency authorized the dredging and removal of millions of pounds of PCB-contaminated sediment from a 40-mile stretch (64.4km) of the Upper Hudson. The action, which was expected to cost more than $780 million, was designed to remove about 250,000 pounds (113,398kg) of PCBs from 490 acres (198ha) of riverbed. Although this amount is less than 20 percent of the Pyranol that the EPA believes was dumped in the Hudson, according to the agency, the "actions in the Upper Hudson will lower the risks to people, fish, and wildlife in the Lower Hudson."[15]

General Electric began the mitigation efforts in 2009, more than 25 years after the EPA designated the Upper Hudson as one of the nation's worst Superfund sites. However, environmentalists point out that the EPA is cleaning up only a relatively small portion of the river bottom. As Gargill explains, "Culling . . . sediment 'hot spots' looks extremely inadequate, and is unlikely to result in the type of permanent solution Superfund law requires, because the valley holding the river in its palm is saturated with untold tons of migrating toxins that threaten to nullify the EPA's nearly $1 billion cure."[16] Whatever the outcome, the story of GE, PCBs, and the EPA shows how difficult it is to clean up toxic waste when powerful forces in business and government oppose one another.

Are Toxic Waste Cleanup Efforts Working?

66 **Congress must reinstate the polluter pays fees. Without corporate fees to replenish Superfund, there is simply not enough money to do the critical job of cleaning up hundreds of toxic waste sites.** 99

—Stephen Lester and Anne Rabe, "Superfund: In the Eye of the Storm," Center for Health, Environment, and Justice, March 2009. www.besafenet.com.

Lester and Rabe are researchers for the Center for Health, Environment, and Justice.

66 **Proponents of Superfund argue that reinstating the [polluter pays] tax will create incentives for companies not to pollute, but there are already strict environmental laws in place, making this additional excise tax unessential and unwise.** 99

—Nicolas Loris, "Obama's Energy Budget: More Taxes, Higher Prices," Heritage Foundation, March 25, 2009. www.heritage.org.

Loris is a research assistant for the Thomas A. Roe Institute for Economic Policy Studies.

Bracketed quotes indicate conflicting positions.

* Editor's Note: While the definition of a primary source can be narrowly or broadly defined, for the purposes of Compact Research, a primary source consists of: 1) results of original research presented by an organization or researcher; 2) eyewitness accounts of events, personal experience, or work experience; 3) first-person editorials offering pundits' opinions; 4) government officials presenting political plans and/or policies; 5) representatives of organizations presenting testimony or policy.

66 Superfund is desperately short of money to clean up abandoned waste sites . . . that continue to menace the environment and, quite often, the health of nearby residents.99

—Joaquin Sapien, "Superfund Today," Center for Public Integrity, April 26, 2007. http://projects.publicintegrity.org.

Sapien is an environmental analyst for the Center for Public Integrity.

66 We're committed to ensuring that remaining National Priorities List hazardous waste sites are cleaned up to protect the environment and the health of all Americans.99

—U.S. Environmental Protection Agency, Superfund: Cleaning Up the Nation's Hazardous Waste Sites, January 4, 2010. www.epa.gov.

The EPA is a federal agency that oversees environmental policy and enforces environmental laws.

66 The military remains largely exempt from compliance with most [Superfund mitigation orders], and the Environmental Protection Agency, the Pentagon's partner in crime, is working hard to keep it that way.99

—Joshua Frank, "The Pentagon Is America's Biggest Polluter," Alternet, May 12, 2008. www.alternet.org.

Frank is an environmental journalist.

66 The efforts by . . . the Pentagon in recent years to resist EPA cleanup requirements are a thing of the past.99

—Benjamin J. Cardin, "Ft. Meade Tour Release," United States Senate, April 14, 2009. http://cardin.senate.gov.

Cardin is a U.S. senator from Maryland.

66 The start of Hudson River dredging is a symbol of victory for the environment and for its river communities. **99**

—George Pavlou, "First Phase of Hudson River Dredging Project Complete," EPA, November 30, 2009. www.epa.gov.

Pavlou is the acting EPA regional administrator.

---

66 We are performing and paying for the work and will provide the EPA with reimbursement for the Agency's past costs to study the Upper Hudson River and its future costs for project oversight. **99**

—Gary Sheffer, "Hudson River Cleanup," General Electric, 2009. www.ge.com.

Sheffer is executive director of communications and public affairs at General Electric.

---

66 The battle for the Hudson is certainly not won, and there is much more testing and cleanup to be done before the Hudson will be truly swimmable. **99**

—Shannon Weiner, "Swimming in the Hudson River: Will the Water Quality Ever Be Satisfactory?" OnEarth, October 19, 2009. www.onearth.org.

Weiner is a riverkeeper ambassador, one who raises awareness about issues concerning the Hudson River.

Are Toxic Waste Cleanup Efforts Working?

- In Chicago alone, more than **400 dry cleaning establishments** polluted with toxic waste were slated for cleanup in 2010. The EPA adds an average of 40 sites a year to its "construction completion" list.

- The United States has **21 hazardous waste landfills** where material from Superfund sites can be dumped.

- To keep a community informed during a **Superfund cleanup**, the EPA will conduct public meetings and issue public notices through the local media.

- About **130 cleaned up Superfund sites** have been returned to productive use as factories, shopping malls, housing, parks, wildlife preserves, and recreational facilities such as golf courses.

- The world headquarters of Internet communications giant **Netscape** is built on a cleaned up Superfund site in Mountain View, California, that was once heavily contaminated with toxic solvents.

- Only **five incinerators** burn PCBs in the United States. They are in Coffeyville, Kansas; Aragonite and Salt Lake City, Utah; and Port Arthur and Deer Park, Texas.

Reimbursements for Superfund Site Cleanups Have Declined

Under the Superfund program, companies deemed responsible for creating a toxic waste site were to repay the government for clean-up costs. In 2007 the Center for Public Integrity released results of an investigation showing that the amount of money the EPA recovered from those companies has significantly declined since 2000. The investigation found that recovered costs peaked in 1998 and 1999, at about $320 million each year. By 2006, the collected recoveries had dropped well below the $100 million mark.

The Superfund sometimes pays for cleanups, which will be paid back later by responsible parties. "Cost recovery" has been declining.

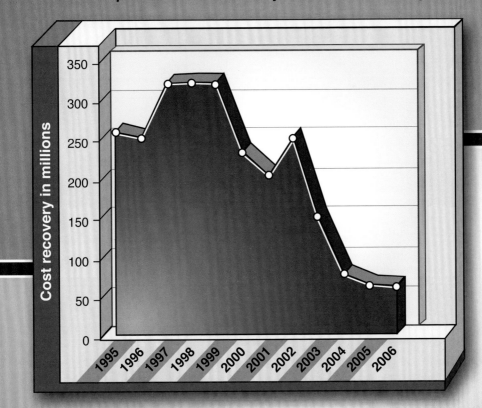

Source: The Center for Public Integrity, "Superfund Today: Massive Undertaking to Clean Up Hazardous Waste Sites Has Lost Both Momentum and Funding," April 26, 2007. www.projects.publicintegrity.org.

National Priorities List

The National Priorities List (NPL) is the EPA's list of national priorities among toxic waste sites in the United States and its territories. Each year new sites are proposed and finalized for inclusion on the list as well as deleted once all cleanup goals have been achieved. A partial deletion from the list means that no further action is needed on a portion of a listed site. Construction completions signify sites that have met certain criteria such as the building of a water treatment system or when all cleanup goals have been met.

Action	1993	1994	1995	1996	1997	1998	1999	2000
Sites Proposed for the NPL	52	36	9	27	20	34	37	40
Sites Finalized on the NPL	33	43	31	13	18	17	43	39
Sites Deleted from the NPL	12	13	25	34	32	20	23	19
Milestone	1993	1994	1995	1996	1997	1998	1999	2000
Partial Deletions*	–	–	–	0	6	7	3	5
Construction Completions	68	61	68	64	88	87	85	87

	2001	2002	2003	2004	2005	2006	2007	2008	2009	2010
	45	9	14	26	12	10	17	17	23	0
	29	19	20	11	18	11	12	18	20	3
	30	17	9	16	18	7	7	9	8	2
	2001	2002	2003	2004	2005	2006	2007	2008	2009	2010
	4	7	7	7	5	3	3	3	3	1
	47	42	40	40	40	40	24	30	20	2

Note: Years shown are fiscal years, October 1 through September 30.
Fiscal year 2010 includes actions and milestones achieved from October 1, 2009 to early 2010.
Partial deletion totals are not applicable until fiscal year 1996, when the policy was first implemented.
* These totals represent the total number of partial deletions by fiscal year and may include multiple partial deletions at a site. Currently, there are 64 partial deletions at 52 sites.

Source: United States Environmental Protection Agency, "National Priorities List," December 15, 2009. www.epa.gov.

- In 2008 the **Pentagon** was voluntarily cleaning up 126 of the 225 military sites on the Superfund list.

- Between 1998 and 2005, companies linked to more than 600 of the nation's most dangerous toxic waste sites spent more than **$1 billion** lobbying politicians and fighting federal agencies to delay cleanup efforts.

- A **multilayered cap** placed over a toxic waste site will usually last for at least 20 years, but with proper maintenance it might last longer.

- In 1983 the EPA declared a 200-mile stretch (322km) of the **Hudson River**, from Hudson Falls to New York City, a Superfund site, and ordered cleanup efforts.

- The **PCB-laden sediment** dredged from the Hudson River, which is expected to fill 4,000 rail cars, is being shipped by train to a toxic dump site in Andrews County, Texas.

How Big a Threat Is Electronic Waste?

In the city of Guiyu, China, dozens of small business owners recycle electronic waste, or e-waste, in their backyards. Coal fires are used to melt the lead solder in circuit boards. The lead is poured into trenches, and the circuit boards are treated with corrosive hydrochloric acid which leaches minute amounts of gold from the equipment. Plastic computer cases, which have no value, are burned in open fires, releasing dioxins and other highly toxic compounds. One unnamed worker commented on the health hazards associated with his recycling job, "The air I breathe in every day is so pungent I can definitely feel it in my windpipe and affecting my lungs. It makes me cough all the time."[17]

Scientists who have studied Guiyu residents report that pregnant women miscarry at a rate that is six times higher than normal. Children as young as five years old work as recyclers, and 70 percent of those studied had dangerously high levels of lead in their blood. After studying the situation, Allen Hershkowitz, a senior scientist and authority on waste management at the Natural Resources Defense Council (NRDC), says, "We have a situation where we have 21st century toxics being managed in a 17th century environment."[18]

A Growing Problem

E-waste is one of the fastest-growing forms of toxic waste. Worldwide, an estimated 20 to 50 million tons (18.1 million to 45.4 million metric tons) of e-waste is discarded annually. About 3 million tons (2.7 million metric tons) of that e-waste is generated in the United States. The discarded electronics that made up American e-waste in 2008 included 30 million desktop computers, 12 million laptops, 32 million computer monitors, 25 million televisions, and 140 million cell phones. In addition, 400 million other devices, including DVD players, game consoles, stereo systems, telephones, and MP3 players, were taken out of service.

> **The United States has few laws that regulate shipping of e-waste to developing nations.**

The e-waste problem is expected to grow since computers, smart phones, and other electronic devices being built today quickly become obsolete. As *National Geographic* staff writer Chris Carroll explains in the 2008 article "High Tech Trash":

> At this very moment, heavily caffeinated software engineers are designing programs that will overtax and befuddle your new turbo-powered PC when you try running them a few years from now. The memory and graphics requirements of Microsoft's recent Vista operating system, for instance, spell doom for aging machines that were still able to squeak by a year ago.[19]

In the United States a large amount of outdated electronic equipment is stored in closets, basements, and garages where it gathers dust. The EPA estimates that approximately 235 million TVs, computers, and other electronic devices sold between 1980 and 2007 are in storage. The

EPA classifies these electronics as ready for "end-of-life management," meaning they will soon be thrown away or recycled.

Recycling Takes Place in Developing Nations

Typically, when the useful life of an electronic device ends, people throw it in the garbage. In the United States about 85 percent of obsolete electronics end up in landfills each year. The other 15 percent, or approximately a billion pounds, are recycled. The market for recycled e-waste is growing because of the valuable contents of circuit boards, also called microchips or chips. Circuit boards perform countless computerized functions in nearly every electronic device from tiny USB flash drives to computers, smartphones, and LCD flat panel TVs. The chips contain gold, silver, copper, and other precious metals. And recycling the metals from old circuit boards is cheaper and easier than obtaining those metals through destructive hard rock mining. However, old electronics contain toxic substances such as lead, arsenic, mercury, and chromium.

Much of the work of recycling the world's e-waste—nearly 70 percent—takes place in China, India, and other developing nations in Southeast Asia and Africa. The United States sends 50 to 80 percent of all e-waste collected for recycling to other countries. The European Union exports about 50 percent of its e-waste. The work of recycling generally falls to impoverished workers who harvest and sell copper wires, circuit boards, and other valuables from massive piles of plastic, metal, and glass that arrive daily in large shipping containers. In May 2009 environmental journalist Tom Zeller Jr. described typical third-world recycling operations as "toxic ecosystems . . . where acrid plumes of smoke rise from circuit-board smelting pits, and children bustle amid a soup of dioxins and mercury leaking from mountains of smoldering electronic trash."[20]

E-Waste Shipping Laws

The United States has few laws that regulate shipping of e-waste to developing nations. According to a report from the Government Accountability Office (GAO) for the House Foreign Affairs Committee,

> A substantial quantity [of exported used electronics] ends up in countries where the items are handled and disposed of in a manner that threatens human health and the envi-

ronment. . . . Federal agencies are not required to track the ultimate destination of . . . donated or recycled e-waste [and therefore] have little assurance that e-waste is ultimately disposed of in an environmentally responsible manner.[21]

An international treaty, called the Basel Convention, was created by the United Nations in 1989 to stop the international toxic waste trade. Katharina Kummer Peiry, the executive secretary of the convention notes that when the treaty was drawn up, "E-waste did not even exist as a waste stream . . . and now it's one of the largest and growing exponentially."[22]

The Basel Convention contains a series of regulations that govern the shipment of hazardous waste. Signed by 170 countries, the accord requires the 29 wealthiest, most industrialized countries to notify developing nations about hazardous waste shipments destined for their shores. However, the notification system had no enforcement provisions, and the law was seen as weak. After protests by environmental groups and activists in developing nations, the law was amended in 1995 with the Basel Ban. This law completely forbids hazardous waste and e-waste shipments to poor countries.

> "The United States is the only industrialized nation that has not agreed to limit exports of toxins to developing nations."

Industrialized nations in the European Union reacted to the Basel Ban by writing the requirements of the accord into their laws, making transfer of e-waste to developing nations illegal. The EU also began requiring manufacturers to produce "green" devices that limit the use of lead, mercury, fire retardants, and other toxic substances. In addition, manufacturers in the EU are required to collect e-waste and recycle it in a safe and responsible manner. But, as Carroll writes, "In spite of these safeguards, untold tons of e-waste still slip out of European ports, on their way to the developing world."[23]

In the United States, powerful forces, such as the Chamber of Commerce, the electronics industry, and the Institute of Scrap Recycling Industries, strongly opposed the Basel Ban. Political pressure from such groups prevented the United States from signing the ban. As a result, the United States is the only industrialized nation that has not agreed to limit exports of toxic waste to developing nations.

The EPA only regulates the export of CRTs in old TVs and monitors. But an undercover investigation by the GAO showed that 43 U.S. recycling firms were shipping old monitors to China, India, Indonesia, and Western Africa without notifying the EPA. The GAO report said, "EPA records show that none of the recyclers . . . had filed proper notifications of their intent to export CRTs for recycling as is required. . . . Some of these seemingly noncompliant companies actively cultivate an environmentally responsible public image; at least three of them held Earth Day 2008 electronics recycling events."[24]

China Deals with E-Waste

The U.S. Environmental Protection Agency estimates that it is up to 10 times cheaper to export e-waste than to dispose of it domestically. As a result, shipping containers filled with old, broken, and out-of-date electronic devices crowd the ports of Kenya, Ghana, India, and China. Stopping the influx is difficult for several reasons, according to Ruediger Kuehr, director of Solving the E-Waste Problem in Bonn, Germany: "China, like India and many other countries, is really hungry for resources, so they let e-waste into their country to support their production chain. They have many people making their living off of e-waste, so they cannot easily say 'Let's stop all of these imports.'"[25]

The Chinese government passed a law banning the import of e-waste in 2002. However, corrupt officials are bribed by recyclers to look the other way as e-waste continues to pour into the country. To deal with the e-waste problem the Chinese government created new mandates in 2009. Funding was set aside to enlarge and improve electronics recycling facilities so they could safely handle e-waste. In addition, manufacturers, retailers, and repair service providers are being asked to handle

> While it is illegal to import e-waste into India, the ministry of environment admits that it is impossible to control the practice.

e-waste responsibly. However, critics charge that the wording of the law is vague, and there are few punitive measures for not complying with the regulations.

E-Waste in India

India also faces a growing mountain of e-waste. A 2008 government study showed that the amount of electronic waste in the country was growing at a rate of 10 percent every year. And 95 percent of the waste, 478,000 tons (434,000 metric tons), will likely end up in urban slums. While it is illegal to import e-waste into India, the ministry of environment admits that it is impossible to control the practice.

The recycling trade is attractive to many of India's poor because a single worker can be self-employed as an e-waste trader, scrap dealer, or computer disassembler. No sophisticated machinery is needed to make money as a recycler, and personal protective equipment is not required for the extraction of valuable materials. Most of the work is done with hammers, screwdrivers, and bare hands.

In Delhi, the recycling trade employs about 25,000 people, with similar numbers in Mumbai and Bangalore. Often whole families do the work. Like recyclers in other developing nations, those in India remove gold from computer chips with cyanide. However, this is a very inefficient process. A large desktop computer contains only 250 parts per million of gold by weight, while a calculator has only 50 parts per million. And the highly poisonous cyanide process retrieves barely 20 percent of the gold. Bharati Chaturvedi, founder of Chintan, a group that works to educate and train India's e-waste workers, spoke to a recycler about the hazardous practices and was told, "I know this is really toxic. . . . It might kill me, I know that. But what shall I do about feeding my children?"[26]

The Path of Least Resistance

Steps are being taken to regulate the recycling business in India and China. But as long as e-waste is created, it will continue to pour into developing nations. David N. Pellow, an ethnic studies professor who examines the social justice aspects of the e-waste trade explains, "It doesn't help in a global sense for one place like China, or India, to become restrictive. The flow simply shifts as it takes the path of least resistance to the bottom."[27] In 2009 that bottom was West Africa, where extreme poverty, corruption, and weak governments make e-waste concerns a very low priority.

When *National Geographic's* Carroll visited e-waste recyclers in Accra, Ghana, he found a price tag on one of the monitors from a Goodwill charity store in Frederick, Maryland. The old monitor, containing about 7 pounds (3kg) of lead, was donated to Goodwill and then purchased by a man named Baah in Alexandria, Virginia. Carroll writes:

> [He] turns out not to be some shady character . . . but a maintenance man in an apartment complex, working 15-hour days fixing toilets and lights. To make ends meet, he tells me, he works nights and weekends exporting used computers to Ghana through his brother. . . . Baah's little exporting business is just one trickle in the cataract of e-waste flowing out of the U.S. and the rest of the developed world.[28]

> "The reality is that manufacturing electronics requires a massive amount of hazardous chemicals that wind up polluting the earth."

Health Problems Increase Massively

A 2008 Greenpeace report on e-waste dumps in Ghana confirmed that high levels of lead, dioxins, and phthalates used in plastic are present in soils and the water near recycling operations. As Kim Schoppink, toxics campaigner at Greenpeace, states, "The pollution and related health problems in countries where e-waste is dumped will increase massively as the amount of electronics used worldwide is growing exponentially and the number of countries used as dump sites will grow."[29] And because it is unprofitable to recycle e-waste in wealthy countries, black clouds of toxic smoke from burning computer parts will be hanging over developing nations for many years to come.

How Big a Threat Is Electronic Waste?

Primary Source Quotes

66 **Hazardous [e-]waste causes long-term poisoning of soil and water, affecting people's health and living conditions. Increasingly unscrupulous trade in waste, which is criminal . . . has become a serious concern.** 99

—Katharina Kummer Peiry, "It Is Time to Stop Environmental Crime at the Border," World Customs Organization, February 2009. http://www.wcoomd.org.

Peiry is in the secretariat of the Basel Convention, which regulates international shipping of e-waste.

66 **If done responsibly, electronics recycling provides a number of environmental benefits.** 99

—Robin Wiener, "Raising the Electronics Recycling Bar in China," *Huffington Post*, December 3, 2008. www.huffingtonpost.com.

Wiener is president of the Institute of Scrap Recycling Industries.

* Editor's Note: While the definition of a primary source can be narrowly or broadly defined, for the purposes of Compact Research, a primary source consists of: 1) results of original research presented by an organization or researcher; 2) eyewitness accounts of events, personal experience, or work experience; 3) first-person editorials offering pundits' opinions; 4) government officials presenting political plans and/or policies; 5) representatives of organizations presenting testimony or policy.

66 **Corporations and management are responsible for the hazardous wastes their companies generate and there are real environmental dangers associated with discarded electrical and electronic equipment.** 99

—Joseph C. Yob Jr., "How to Prevent IT Assets from Becoming IT Liabilities: Why You Need a Plan to Manage Your IT Assets Through Their Life Cycle," Creative Recycling, 2009. www.crserecycling.com.

Yob is vice president of Creative Recycling Systems, Inc.

66 **All the e-waste we collect in North America is processed in the U.S., and nothing is shipped overseas for disposal. . . . We hold our recycling vendors to the highest environmental standards in the industry.** 99

—Steve Jobs, "A Greener Apple," Apple, 2009. www.apple.com.

Jobs is CEO of Apple, Inc.

66 **Almost every time an e-waste dismantler has shown me around his premises, he has pointed out imported waste. Big global brand names sit like surreal ads among these heaps.** 99

—Bharati Chaturvedi, "Dismantling India's E-Waste: Potential for Green Jobs?" *Huffington Post*, November 24, 2009. www.huffingtonpost.com.

Chaturvedi is the founder of Chintan, a group that organizes India's e-waste recyclers.

66 **Nokia is encouraging the recycling of unwanted devices through a series of campaigns and activities, providing information on how to go about recycling old devices, chargers and other mobile accessories.** 99

—Gopal Krishna, "Separate Legislation for E-Waste Management Facts," ToxicsWatch, August 2, 2008. http://toxicswatch.blogspot.com.

Krishna is an Indian environmental health analyst.

> **There [are] already more than half a billion old phones sitting in American drawers. That added up to more than $300 million worth of gold, palladium, silver, copper and platinum.**

—Jon Mooallem, "The Afterlife of Cellphones," *New York Times*, January 13, 2008. www.nytimes.com.

Mooallem is an environmental correspondent for the *New York Times*.

> **We as consumers have to be responsible for our ignorance. [We] have to think, 'what happens to this product when it dies?'**

—Jim Puckett, "The Dark Side of the Information Age," *Frontline*, 2009. www.pbs.org.

Puckett is founder of the Basel Action Network.

How Big a Threat Is Electronic Waste?

- E-waste contains **toxic metals and chemicals** which affect blood systems, kidneys, the brain and spleen, and also cause skin diseases, cancer, neurological and respiratory disorders, and birth defects.

- Americans bought **2.9 million HDTVs** for the 2009 Super Bowl and a total of 34.5 million digital TVs for the entire year.

- Guiyu, China, is home to **5,500 e-waste recycling businesses** that contribute **$75 million** a year to the local economy.

- In the United States about **85 percent** of obsolete electronics are sent to landfills while only **15 percent** are recycled.

- European consumers create **8.7 million tons** (7.9 million metric tons) of e-waste each year.

- China's National Statistical Bureau expects the amount of e-waste created domestically to grow **5 to 10 percent annually**.

- More than **500 shipping containers**, each containing 10 to 15 tons (9.1 to 13.6 metric tons) of e-waste, enter Nigerian ports every month.

- One ton (0.9 metric tons) of scrap from a discarded computer contains more **gold** than can be produced from 17 tons (15.4 metric tons) of gold ore.

Asia Gets Much of the World's Electronic Waste

Developed countries send much of their e-waste to developing countries in Asia, often in violation of international law. India and China are among the biggest recipients of e-waste, although China banned the import of e-waste in 2002. E-waste recycling can yield valuable substances such as copper, iron, and gold. A mobile phone, for instance, is 19 percent copper and 8 percent iron. But e-waste also contains hazardous substances that can harm workers in recycling yards and nearby residents, few of whom are protected by laws.

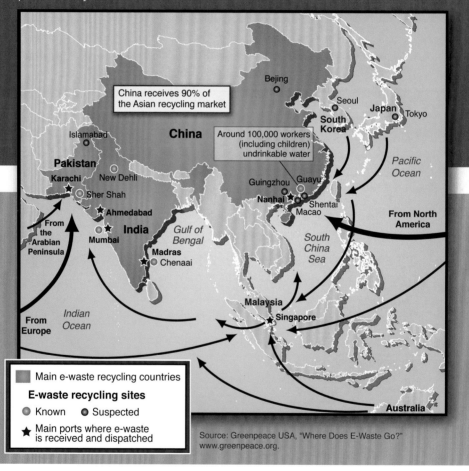

China receives 90% of the Asian recycling market

Around 100,000 workers (including children) undrinkable water

Main e-waste recycling countries

E-waste recycling sites
○ Known ◉ Suspected
★ Main ports where e-waste is received and dispatched

Source: Greenpeace USA, "Where Does E-Waste Go?" www.greenpeace.org.

- Although the European Union strictly bans e-waste exports, over **6.6 million tons** (6 million metric tons) of discarded electronics are shipped from the EU to Africa every year.

Some States Say No to E-Waste Disposal

Concerns about human health and climate change have prompted some U.S. states and at least one city to pass laws prohibiting electronic devices from being incinerated or dumped in landfills. Twelve U.S. states and New York City have passed such laws. At the same time, more states now require e-waste recycling.

Landfill or Incineration Ban

No Landfill or Incineration Ban

Source: Electronic Recyclers International, Inc., "U.S. Landfill Ban." http://electronicrecyclers.com.

- Of the **140 million cell phones** taken out of service every year in the United States only **10 percent** are recycled.

- Each cell phone contains about **$1** worth of precious metals, mostly gold.

E-Waste Recycling Threatens Human Health and the Environment in China

Cheap labor and weak laws have made China a top location for e-waste recycling. In Guiyu, China, investigators have observed recyclers handling and processing all manner of hazardous electronics components. Computer wires, for instance, are

Computer/ E-Waste Component	Process Witnessed in Guiyu, China
Cathode ray tubes (CRTs)	Breaking, removal of copper yoke, and dumping
Printed circuit boards	De-soldering and removing computer chips
Dismantled printed circuit board processing	Open burning of waste boards that have had chips removed to remove final metals
Chips and other gold-plated components	Chemical stripping using nitric and hydrochloric acids along riverbanks
Plastics from computers and peripherals, e.g. printers, keyboards, etc.	Shredding and low-temperature melting to be reutilized in poor-grade plastics
Computer wires	Open burning to recover copper
Miscellaneous computer parts encased in rubber or plastic; e.g. steel rollers	Open burning to recover steel and other metals
Toner cartridges	Use of paint brushes to recover toner without any protection
Secondary steel or copper and precious metal smelting	Furnace recovers steel or copper from waste, including organics

burned out in the open to recover valuable copper, exposing workers and their families to carcinogenic substances and releasing toxic ash into the air, water, and soil.

Potential Occupational Hazard	Potential Environmental Hazard
• Silicosis • Cuts from CRT glass in case of implosion • Inhalation or contact with phosphor containing cadmium or other metals	• Lead, barium and other heavy metals leaching into groundwater, release of toxic phosphor
• Tin and lead inhalation • Possible brominated dioxin, beryllium, cadmium, mercury inhalation	• Air emission of same substances
• Toxicity to workers and nearby residents from tin, lead, brominated dioxin, beryllium, cadmium, and mercury inhalation • Respiratory irritation	• Tin and lead contamination of immediate environment, including surface and groundwaters. • Brominated dioxins, beryllium, cadmium, and mercury emissions
• Acid contact with eyes, skin may result in permanent injury • Inhalation of mists and fumes of acids, chlorine, and sulphur dioxide gases can cause respiratory irritation to severe effects, including pulmonary edema, circulatory failure, and death	• Hydrocarbons, heavy metals, brominated substances, etc., discharged directly into rivers and banks. • Acidifies the river, destroying fish and flora
• Probable hydrocarbon, brominated dioxin, and heavy metal exposures	• Emissions of brominated dioxins and heavy metals and hydrocarbons
• Brominated and chlorinated dioxin, polycyclic aromatic hydrocarbons (PAH) (carcinogenic) exposure to workers living in the burning works area	• Hydrocarbon ashes including PAHs discharged into air, water, and soil
• Hydrocarbon including PAHs and potential dixoic exposure	• Hydrocarbon ashes including PAHs discharged into air, water, and soil
• Respiratory tract irritation • Carbon black possible human carcinogen • Cyan, yellow, and magenta toners unknown toxicity	• Cyan, yellow, and magenta toners unknown toxicity
• Exposure to dioxins and heavy metals	• Emissions of dioxins and heavy metals

Source: The Basel Action Network and Silicon Valley Toxins Coalition, "Exporting Harm: The Hi-Tech Trashing of Asia," February 25, 2002.

What Is the Future of Toxic Waste?

> 66 We must encourage innovation in green chemistry, and support research, education, recognition, and other strategies that will lead us down the road to safer and more sustainable chemicals and processes. 99
>
> —Lisa P. Jackson, administrator of the EPA.

> 66 Funding to study green chemistry and to develop benign chemistry . . . remains sparse. 99
>
> —Hannah Hoag, environmental journalist.

Because some types of toxic waste take decades to degrade and others persist in the environment even longer, experts agree that hazardous waste will be with us for a very long time. But that does not mean that attitudes toward toxic waste have stayed the same. In recent years, knowledge about toxic waste has increased, and awareness of the health and environmental problems it causes has grown as well. People have come to understand the importance of reducing the use of hazardous chemicals in manufacturing and agriculture, and scientists are searching for better ways to store or dispose of hazardous waste. The future of toxic waste lies in efforts to accomplish these goals, along with developing safer and more efficient reuse and recycling programs.

States Tackle E-Waste

According to a November 2009 poll by Pike Research, 76 percent of American consumers see recycling as the key to reducing the world's e-waste, and 63 percent of consumers said they were willing to pay a small amount for e-waste recycling services. This view is evident in the surge of e-waste laws passed in about 20 states between 2003 and 2009. California was the first state to tackle the e-waste problem with the Electronic Waste Recycling Act of 2003. The law, which went into effect in January 2004, initially designated TVs and computer monitors made with cathode ray tubes as hazardous waste. To pay for collection and recycling of old equipment, consumers are charged a small fee (it was $8 to $15 in 2009) when they purchase new TVs or monitors. In 2005, laptop computers and devices with LCD screens larger than 4 inches were also subject to the recycling fee. In 2006 consumers were also required to recycle batteries. The following year the law mandated that TVs, computers, and other electronics sold in the state could not contain more than .01 percent by weight of cadmium, hexavalent chromium, lead, or mercury.

The California law is unique because it is the only e-waste law that charges consumers for recycling. The other state laws contain what are called producer responsibility requirements. These laws, called take back initiatives, require electronics producers to pay for the collection, transportation, and recycling of e-waste. In some cases, towns and cities provide collection points for e-waste. The laws ensure that all recycled goods are handled properly and none are shipped to developing nations.

The state of Washington has one of the most comprehensive e-waste laws and includes strict take back requirements. Enacted in 2009, Washington's E-Cycle Program provides free recycling to anyone wishing to dispose of televisions, computers, monitors, and other equipment. The law requires electronics manufacturers to pay the cost of the recycling program.

> People have come to understand the importance of reducing the use of hazardous chemicals in manufacturing and agriculture, and scientists are searching for better ways to store or dispose of hazardous waste.

Measures Involving Electronics Manufacturers

Many large electronics manufacturers, including Dell, Epson, and IBM, have instituted their own recycling programs. And in 2009 the trade organization Electronic Industries Alliance was working with Canon, Hewlett Packard, JVC, Kodak, Nokia, Panasonic, Philips Electronics, Sharp, and Sony to initiate electronics collection and recycling programs. For example, Sony has partnered with Waste Management to provide locations where unwanted Sony products can be dropped off and recycled for free.

At the same time, the European Union has sought to become a global leader in regulating hazardous chemicals and e-waste. Two laws adopted by the EU in 2002, known as the Waste from Electrical and Electronic Equipment (WEEE) and the Restriction on Hazardous Substances (RoHS), require electronics manufacturers to handle their own e-waste while eliminating certain hazardous substances from the production process. The WEEE regulations cover a wide range of products that must be recycled, including computers, TVs, hair dryers, refrigerators, and electronic toys. The RoHS restrictions banned toxic substances commonly used in manufacturing, including lead, cadmium, mercury, hexavalent chromium, and brominated flame retardants. As a result of RoHS, electronics manufacturers, including those in the United States, were forced to remove toxic chemicals from their products so that they could be sold in EU countries.

> " The [EU] banned toxic substances commonly used in manufacturing, including lead, cadmium, mercury, hexavalent chromium, and brominated flame retardants. "

Research shows that computers from EU nations still end up in developing nations. However, EU authorities hope that banning commonly used hazardous chemicals will at least make the future of third-world recycling less toxic.

While manufacturers work to reduce their toxic footprint, millions of pounds of e-waste continue to pile up every day. In India, Bharati Chaturvedi started a creative new organization called Chintan to deal with this problem. Chintan is working to set up a union of computer dismantlers who will come together under one roof to safely and legally recycle old circuit boards, monitors, and related equipment. The first dismantling factory was scheduled to open in Delhi in 2010, and Chaturvedi hopes that this model can spread to other cities, as he explains: "If the informal [recycling] systems continue, they will always be cheaper than any formal system and [new recycling] rules will be hard to implement. The trick lies in working with today's informal workers—the ones who currently take apart our [e-waste]. They can be organized, registered and helped into safe workplaces."[30]

> " Chintan is working to set up a union of computer dismantlers who will come together under one roof to safely and legally recycle old circuit boards, monitors, and related equipment. "

Chintan has received a boost from the Indian government, which is creating rules to force electronics producers to take responsibility for handling the end-of-life management of their products. The Indian laws will also force big, global manufacturers to change their production practices in order to eliminate toxic chemicals. Commenting on the regulations, Chaturvedi states, "Such rules change the game considerably. Often, manufacturers shudder at such state-imposed obligations. But it's also a historic opportunity for them to clean up high-tech toxics. . . . They can ensure they are part of the solution."[31]

E-waste recycling remains largely unregulated in much of China. However, in Beijing, the nation's capital, officials began setting up a network of e-waste recycling centers in 2009. When the project is completed, the centers will have the capability of safely dismantling and recycling about 100,000 electronic devices and major appliances every month.

China is also planning to impose producer responsibility rules on manufacturers. One company is taking the initiative to control the e-waste created by sales of its products before any such laws go into effect. The TV maker Changhong, based in the western province of Sichuan, has made plans to open China's largest TV recycling facility. In 2009 the company invested about $1 million to develop and build equipment needed for recycling, and the plant was expected to open by 2011.

Green Chemistry

In the United States the future of toxic chemical waste is being determined in legislative bodies and laboratories. And the push for new laws is inspiring researchers to devise greener methods for producing plastics and other polluting substances.

In 2008 the most comprehensive toxic waste laws in the nation were signed by governor Arnold Schwarzenegger of California. The Green Chemistry Initiative (GCI), scheduled to be enacted over the course of 10 years, consists of two laws that force manufacturers that do business in the state to replace toxic chemicals with safer alternatives. The GCI is based on the Precautionary Principle, which regulates chemicals even though uncertainties exist concerning their effect on the environment or health. The chemicals, many of which generate toxic waste, include those used in fuel, building materials, and retail items. Upon signing the GCI, Schwarzenegger explained the benefits of the legislation, saying, "It . . . puts an end to the less effective 'chemical-by-chemical' bans of the past. With these . . . bills, we will stop looking at toxics as an inevitable by-product of industrial production. Instead they will be something that can be removed from every product in the design stage—protecting people's health and our environment."[32]

> " In the United States the future of toxic chemical waste is being determined in legislative bodies and laboratories. "

Maureen Gorsen, former head of California's Department of Toxic Substances Control (DTSC) said the idea of the initiative is to have products designed to be "green at the molecular level"[33] so they do not damage the environment as they are created or discarded. These laws, "will govern how business will be conducted in California for the next 20 or 30 years."[34] Gorsen said the law is urgently needed because California's $7 billion-a-year chemical industry is expected to double production every 25 years.

Some industries oppose broad regulations like those adopted in California. For example, the Grocery Manufacturers Association asked the DTSC to limit its oversight to the small number of chemicals that are known to be hazardous instead of using the Precautionary Principle to eliminate hundreds of suspected substances. According to the grocery association, the state should concentrate on "the important few" chemicals versus the "trivial many."[35] Despite such requests, California is planning to implement the comprehensive initiative by 2018.

Recognizing Achievement

The idea for the California Green Chemistry Initiative came from an EPA program enacted in 1995 called the Presidential Green Chemistry Challenge Award. This program provides presidential recognition to scientists and companies who invent eco-friendly products and processes. One of the five winners in 2008, professor Krzysztof Matyjaszewski at Pittsburgh's Carnegie Mellon University, invented a complex process called atom transfer radical polymerization or ATRP. This process, used in making adhesives, coatings, and medical products, uses ascorbic acid, also known as vitamin C, to replace synthetic polymers in the manufacturing process.

Since the Presidential Green Chemistry Challenge Award was initiated, many highly toxic chemicals have been eliminated. For example, in 2002 scientists at NatureWorks devised a method for using a corn-based chemical called PLA to produce plastics used in textiles and food packaging. Since that time, Wal-Mart has been integrating PLA into its packaging process. The new plastic packages are recyclable, can be composted, and do not leach toxic chemicals into the environment like traditional plastic polymers.

> **Oyster mushrooms are highly efficient at restoring soil polluted by oil and gasoline.**

The PLA and ATRP processes, along with other procedures devised through the Presidential Green Chemistry Challenge Award, have eliminated the production of more than 1.3 billion pounds (0.6 billion kg) of hazardous chemicals and solvents used in the making of polymers for plastic. However, this is only a small percentage of the approximately 400 billion pounds (181.4 billion kg) of synthetic polymers that are produced each year.

Mushrooms and Microbes

While some scientists are working on ways to reduce toxic waste in the future, others are devising new methods to clean up Superfund sites. For example, Paul Stamets, a mushroom expert, or mycologist, has demonstrated that oyster mushrooms are highly efficient at restoring soil polluted by oil and gasoline. In one test, the cobweb-like underground growth of the oyster mushroom, called mycelium, devoured 95 percent of the toxins at a site polluted by diesel fuel. And when placed around rivers or lakes, the mycelium also filtered toxic waste from pesticide and fertilizer runoff.

Like the mushroom mycelium, certain microbes can eat up toxic waste in seriously polluted areas. A bacterium known as BAV1, for example, flourishes in soil polluted by vinyl chloride, the most common and hazardous industrial chemical. The bacterium was discovered 20 feet below the surface at a toxic waste site in Oscoda, Michigan, where BAV1 was eating the toxic compound, rendering it harmless. People are exposed to vinyl chloride when it seeps into aquifers and ends up in the drinking water supply. Those exposed to vinyl chloride may suffer from dizziness, headaches, and liver cancer. It is found at about one-third of Superfund sites and lingers in the soil for hundreds of years.

Scientists are hoping to isolate the enzyme within the bacterium that breaks down the vinyl chloride. This could be used to genetically modify the bacterium to eat other toxic substances. This process, called bioremediation, is on the cutting edge of science. But finding new living organisms to reduce or eliminate environmental hazards is a slow process requiring the extensive study of millions of microbes. While problems need to be surmounted, those who discover new ways to clean up toxic waste can reap huge financial rewards. Every year billions of dollars are spent by government and private industry to clean up hazardous chemicals. With so much money available to those who provide solutions, microbes and mushrooms will likely play an important role in the never-ending quest for a cleaner planet.

What Is the Future of Toxic Waste?

66 India is close to finalizing the world's strictest set of rules on disposing of electronic waste. The rules are now being given the final touch by the Ministry of Environment and Forests. 99

—Gopal Krishna, "Separate Legislation for E-Waste Management Facts," ToxicsWatch, August 2, 2008.
http://toxicswatch.blogspot.com.

Krishna is an Indian environmental health analyst.

66 Despite the tough restrictions . . . companies ship electronics [to developing nations] that still contain high concentrations of two hazardous substances— hexavalent chromium . . . and the brominated flame retardant. 99

—Steve Jobs, "A Greener Apple," Apple, 2009. www.apple.com.

Jobs is CEO of Apple, Inc.

* Editor's Note: While the definition of a primary source can be narrowly or broadly defined, for the purposes of Compact Research, a primary source consists of: 1) results of original research presented by an organization or researcher; 2) eyewitness accounts of events, personal experience, or work experience; 3) first-person editorials offering pundits' opinions; 4) government officials presenting political plans and/or policies; 5) representatives of organizations presenting testimony or policy.

66 **Enacting national RoHS and WEEE rules [in the United States] is an environmentally responsible thing to do. . . . National RoHS and WEEE laws will provide incentives for removing these substances from new products, and for properly disposing of existing products.** 99

—Paul Tallentire, "Why Federal RoHS and WEEE Laws Are Imperative," Greentech Zone, 2009. www.en-genius.net.

Tallentire is president of Newark InOne, an electronic component distributor.

66 **Much of the chemistry that the industry currently uses is decades old and from a time that environmental protection was an afterthought, if it was a thought at all.** 99

—Rich Engler, "Green Chemistry—Chemistry Done Right," Greenversations, June 23, 2009. http://blog.epa.gov.

Engler is the program manager of EPA's Green Chemistry Program.

66 **Businesses, consumers, investors and governments need chemicals and products that have low to no toxicity and degrade into innocuous substances in the environment.** 99

—Mark S. Rossi, "Mr. Maziar Movassaghi. Acting Director. California Department of Toxic Substances Business," Working Group, June 1, 2009. www.bizngo.org.

Rossi is research director for Clean Production Action.

66 **I am excited to [sign the Green Chemistry Initiative], which will spur a new era of research and innovation and promises to drive economic growth and competition in the green chemistry sector.** 99

—Arnold Schwarzenegger, "Governor Schwarzenegger Signs Groundbreaking Legislation Implementing First-in-the-Nation Green Chemistry Program," Office of the Governor, September 29, 2008. http://gov.ca.gov.

Schwarzenegger is governor of California.

66 [The Green Chemical Initiative] will drive California's economy toward the development of safer alternatives for consumer products while simultaneously providing a balanced and sustainable approach. 99

—Curt Augustine, "Maziar Movassaghi, Acting Director," Green Chemistry Alliance, June 26, 2009. www.cicc.org.

Augustine is director of policy and government affairs at the Alliance of Automobile Manufacturers' California office.

....

66 [The] nation's first-ever Green Chemistry Initiative ... is being closely watched by industry and activists as a likely precedent for such initiatives in other states and possibly at the federal level. 99

—Matt Shipman, "California Report Cites TSCA as Green Chemistry Barrier, Urges New Law," California EPA, January 22, 2008. http://coeh.berkeley.edu.

Shipman is managing editor of *Water Policy Report* and a contributing writer for the *Inside EPA Weekly Report*.

....

66 If you really want to be e-green, try this ... don't upgrade your old TV (or phone or computer) for a little while longer. 99

—Bryan Walsh, "E-Waste Not," *Time*, January 8, 2009. www.time.com.

Walsh is an environmental journalist for *Time*.

....

What Is the Future of Toxic Waste?

- In an August 2009 poll conducted by Lake Research Partners **53 percent** of Americans said they would pay more for environmentally friendly televisions made with fewer toxic chemicals.

- Less than **5 percent** of all unwanted personal computers are donated to schools, charities, or nonprofit organizations for reuse.

- Between 2006 and 2008 Dell recycled about **255 million pounds** (115.7 million kg) of its own products.

- In Beijing, China, officials are planning a network of e-waste recycling centers to safely dismantle and recycle **100,000** electronic devices and major appliances every month.

- India has partnered with German and Swiss government organizations to form the **Indo-German-Swiss e-Waste Initiative** meant to educate and train Indian electronics recyclers.

- The Indian organization **Chintan** is setting up schools to help children working as e-waste recyclers become full-time students.

- As of 2008, 35 states of the United States were considering electronic recycling regulations called **"diversion from landfill"** laws that make it illegal to dispose of e-waste in landfills.

- In April 2009 the EPA was authorized to give grants to universities, government labs, and private industries to **conduct research** that will improve recycling and reduction of hazardous materials in electronic devices.

Some States Require the Recycling of E-Waste

Eighteen states have passed laws requiring statewide e-waste recycling and several other states are considering similar legislation. New York City also requires the recycling of e-waste. Except in California, these laws require makers of electronic devices to pay for the costs of e-waste recycling. The California law, known as a Consumer Advanced Recycling Fee law, charges consumers a recycling fee.

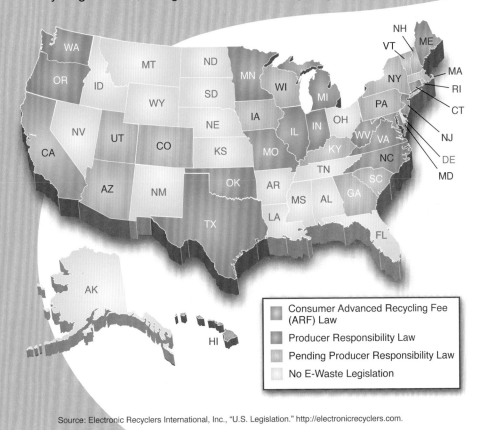

Consumer Advanced Recycling Fee (ARF) Law

Producer Responsibility Law

Pending Producer Responsibility Law

No E-Waste Legislation

Source: Electronic Recyclers International, Inc., "U.S. Legislation." http://electronicrecyclers.com.

- Green Chemistry relies on a set of **12 principles** that can be used to design or redesign molecules, materials, and chemical reactions so they are safer for human health and the environment.

- In 2007 scientist Richard Wool created working circuit boards from a biodegradable chemical made of **chicken feathers and soybeans**.

Americans Worry About Polluted Drinking Water

Pollution of drinking water is the top environmental concern of Americans, according to a 2009 Gallup poll. The poll found that 59 percent of Americans have a "great deal" of concern about pollution of drinking water, followed closely by concerns about pollution of rivers, lakes, and reservoirs and contamination of soil and water by toxic waste. Maintenance of the nation's supply of freshwater for household needs is also of concern.

I'm going to read you a list of environmental problems. As I read each one, please tell me if you personally worry about this problem a great deal, a fair amount, only a little, or not at all. First, how much do you personally worry about . . .?

	Great deal %	Fair amount %	Only a little/Not at all %
Pollution of drinking water	59	25	16
Pollution of rivers, lakes, and reservoirs	52	31	17
Contamination of soil and water by toxic waste	52	28	19
Maintenance of the nation's supply of fresh water for household needs	49	31	19
Air pollution	45	31	24
The loss of tropical rain forests	42	26	32
Extinction of plant and animal species	37	28	34
The "greenhouse effect" or global warming/Global warming	34	26	40

Source: Gallup Poll, "Water Pollution Americans' Top Green Concern," March 25, 2009. www.gallup.com.

United States Has Mixed Recycling Rates

Some products, such as car batteries, have high rates of recycling in the United States while others, such as tires and electronic devices, are recycled much less often, according to 2007 statistics from Electronic Recyclers International. However, recent polls show that Americans see recycling as the key to reducing waste.

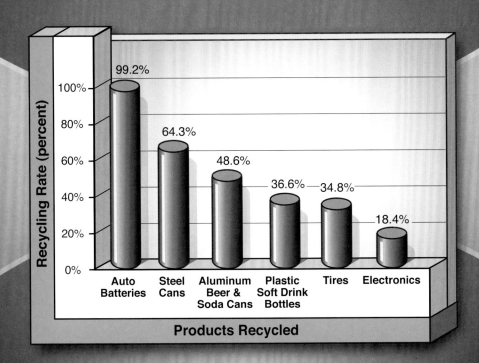

Source: Electronic Recyclers International, Inc., "Recycling Rates of Selected Products in the United States for 2007," 2008. http://electronicrecyclers.com.

- In 2008 the Department of Defense, which has **6,000 toxic dump sites** to clean up, provided a **$381,000** grant to Gene Network Sciences (GNS) to study a microbe that eats chlorine atoms in toxic waste.

- One unique bacterium used to clean up radioactive waste is named *Deinococcus radiodurans*, meaning **"strange berry that withstands radiation."**

Key People and Advocacy Groups

The Basel Action Network (BAN): This group seeks to prevent the dumping of e-waste and other toxic pollutants in developing nations and promotes toxic-free design of consumer products.

Linda S. Birnbaum: As director of the Experimental Toxicology Division at the EPA for 16 years, Birnbaum conducted research into the health effects of environmental pollutants. In 2008 she was named the director of both the National Institute of Environmental Health Sciences and the National Toxicology Program. Birnbaum has written extensively on toxins and their effects on health and the environment.

Dow Chemical Company: As the second largest chemical producer in the world, Dow has 46,000 employees worldwide and annual sales of over $57 billion. Dow produces plastics, chemicals, and agricultural compounds in 175 countries, and these products play an integral role in modern society. According to the EPA, Dow is responsible for 96 of the worst Superfund toxic waste dumps in the United States.

Allen Hershkowitz: Hershkowitz is a senior scientist with the Natural Resources Defense Council. He specializes in issues related to sustainable development, industrial ecology, the paper industry, toxic waste management, and recycling. Hershkowitz has served on the DuPont Corporation's Bio-Based Fuels Life Cycle Assessment Advisory Board, the National Research Council Committee on the Health Effects of Waste Incineration, and the EPA's Science Advisory Board Subcommittee on Sludge Incineration.

The Institute of Scrap Recycling Industries, Inc. (ISRI): The ISRI is a private, nonprofit trade association that calls itself the "Voice of the Recycling Industry." Based in Washington, D.C., ISRI represents more than 1,650 private, for-profit companies that process, broker, and consume scrap commodities, including metals, paper, electronics, rubber, plastics, glass, and textiles.

Lisa Perez Jackson: Jackson is a chemical engineer serving as the administrator of the Environmental Protection Agency. She previously worked as the commissioner for the New Jersey Department of Environmental Protection where she oversaw the cleanup of hazardous waste sites under the Superfund program.

Robert F. Kennedy Jr.: Kennedy represents the Hudson Riverkeeper and Waterkeeper Alliance, groups that led the fight to restore the Hudson River. The group's achievement helped spawn more than 130 Waterkeeper organizations across the globe. Kennedy is the author of numerous books, including the environmental best-seller *Crimes Against Nature* and *The Riverkeepers*.

Katharina Kummer Peiry: Peiry is the executive secretary of the Basel Convention, which regulates the trade in e-waste. As a specialist in international environmental law and policy, Peiry has worked on issues related to the Basel Convention since 1988. She has written extensively on international environmental law, international chemicals and waste management, and other environmental issues.

Silicon Valley Toxics Coalition (SVTC): Formed in 1982 when hazardous waste was discovered in groundwater throughout Silicon Valley near high-tech manufacturing facilities, this organization was instrumental in the EPA's identification of 29 Superfund sites in Silicon Valley for immediate cleanup.

Chronology

1897
The world's second largest chemical manufacturer, Dow Chemical, is founded in Midland, Michigan.

1977
PCB production is banned by the EPA.

1972
Congress creates the Clean Water Act to regulate the types and amounts of toxic waste that industries can dump into lakes, rivers, and oceans.

1900   1950   1970   1975   1980

1942
Hooker Chemical begins using Love Canal, near Niagara Falls, New York, as a toxic waste dump.

1976
Congress passes the Toxic Substances Control Act giving the EPA authority to regulate toxic substances from the "cradle to the grave."

1979
The Valley of the Drums in Kentucky, is a 23-acre (9.3ha) abandoned hazardous waste site containing over 17,000 steel drums filled with highly toxic chemicals, is featured in newspapers across the United States.

1980

Congress enacts the Comprehensive Environmental Response, Compensation and Liability Act (CERCLA), commonly referred to as the Superfund, to clean up industrial waste.

2009

On February 13 Congress passes the American Recovery and Reinvestment Act directing $600 million to speed up cleanup actions at Superfund sites.

1990

The number of Superfund sites on the National Priorities List tops 1,200.

1980   1990   2000   2010

1983

The EPA declares a 200-mile stretch (322km) of the Hudson River a Superfund site.

1995

Congress votes to discontinue the Superfund tax on large polluters such as oil and chemical companies.

2002

The EPA institutes the National Waste Minimization Program to support efforts to reduce toxic waste generation in industry.

Related Organizations

American Chemistry Council

1300 Wilson Blvd.

Arlington, VA 22209

phone: (703) 741-5000 • fax: (703) 741-6050

e-mail: patrick_hurston@americanchemistry.com

Web site: www.americanchemistry.com

The American Chemistry Council represents the leading companies engaged in the business of chemistry. The council's members apply the science of chemistry to make products that are essential to daily life. The council publishes numerous educational brochures about various chemicals and their uses in everyday life.

American Council on Science and Health (ACSH)

1995 Broadway, 2nd Floor

New York, NY 10023-5860

phone: (866) 905-2694 • fax: (212) 362-4919

e-mail: acsh@acsh.org • Web site: www.acsh.org

The American Council on Science and Health is a consumer education group concerned with issues related to food, nutrition, chemicals, the environment, and health. The ACSH is funded by oil producers Chevron and Exxon, food producers such as Frito-Lay and Coca-Cola, and by Dow Chemical and other major chemical manufacturers.

The Center for Public Integrity

910 17th St. NW, Suite 700

Washington, DC 20006

phone: (202) 466-1300

Web site: www.publicintegrity.org

The Center for Public Integrity is dedicated to producing investigative journalism on issues concerning the environment and other important topics. The center generates investigative reports, databases, and analyses and publishes the PaperTrail Blog and the *Daily Watchdog* news report.

Earthworks

1612 K St. NW, Suite 808

Washington, DC 20006

phone: (202) 887-1872

e-mail: info@earthworksaction.org

Web site: www.earthworksaction.org

Earthworks is dedicated to protecting the environment from the impacts of mineral development. The organization works to reform government policies, improve corporate practices, and encourage responsible materials sourcing and consumption. The group publishes the *Earthworks Journal* and the *EarthNotes* newsletter as well as the EARTHblog.

Environmental Defense Fund (EDF)

257 Park Ave. South

New York, NY 10010

phone: (212) 505-2100 • fax: (212) 505-2375

Web site: www.edf.org

The Environmental Defense Fund is a nonprofit organization with more than 700,000 members. Science gathered by the EDF has been at the forefront of historic movements such as the banning of the pesticide DDT in 1967 and the passage of the Safe Drinking Water Act in 1974.

The Environmental Working Group (EWG)

1436 U St. NW, Suite 100

Washington, DC 20009

phone: (202) 667-6982

Web site: www.ewg.org

The Environmental Working Group investigates and publicizes environmental contamination. The group's research exposes polluters and their lobbyists and works with politicians to shape policy on toxic waste and other environmental issues. The EWG publishes the Mulch Blog and the online periodical *AgMag*.

National Mining Association (NMA)

101 Constitution Ave. NW, Suite 500 East

Washington, DC

phone: (202) 463-2600 • fax: (202) 463-2666

e-mail: craulston@nma.org. • Web site: www.nma.org

The National Mining Association is a national trade organization that represents the interests of mining to Congress, the administration, federal agencies, the judiciary, and the media. The NMA's Web site provides numerous publications concerning various minerals, the environment, and facts about mining.

Natural Resources Defense Council (NRDC)

40 W. 20th St.

New York, NY 10011

phone: (212) 727-2700 • fax: (212) 727-1773

e-mail: nrdcinfo@nrdc.org • Web site: www.nrdc.org

The Natural Resources Defense Council uses law, science, and the support of 1.2 million members and online activists to protect the environment. The NRDC publishes *On Earth*, a quarterly magazine; *Nature's Voice*, a bimonthly online magazine; and various reports and e-mail bulletins.

The Pesticide Action Network North America

49 Powell St., Suite 500

San Francisco, CA 94102

phone: (415) 981-1771 • fax: (415) 981-1991

e-mail: panna@panna.org • Web site: www.panna.org

The Pesticide Action Network works to replace the use of hazardous pesticides with ecologically sound alternatives. The organization publishes *PAN North America*, a magazine that covers sustainable food systems and chronicles progress made toward pesticide reform.

Sierra Club

85 Second St., 2nd Floor

San Francisco, CA 94105-3441

phone: (415) 977-5500 • fax: (415) 977-5799

e-mail: information@sierraclub.org • Website: www.sierraclub.org

The Sierra Club is a nonprofit public interest organization that promotes conservation of the natural environment by influencing public policy decisions—legislative, administrative, legal, and electoral. It publishes *Sierra* magazine as well as books on the environment.

Superfund

Environmental Protection Agency

Ariel Rios Bldg., 1200 Pennsylvania Ave. NW

Washington, DC 20460

phone: (800) 424-9346

Web site: www.epa.gov

Superfund is the federal government's program to clean up the nation's uncontrolled hazardous waste sites. The Web site contains information about Superfund sites in every region of the country, the health effects of common contaminants, cleanup efforts, and how citizens can become involved in cleanup activities in their communities.

For Further Research

Books

Dan Agin, *Junk Science*. New York: St. Martin's, 2007.

Phil Brown, *Toxic Exposures*. New York: Columbia University Press, 2008.

Phillip J. Cooper, *The War Against Regulation: From Jimmy Carter to George W. Bush*. Lawrence: University Press of Kansas, 2009.

Bonnie Greene, *Night Fire*. New York: HarperCollins, 2008.

Stefan Kiesbye, *Nuclear and Toxic Waste*. Detroit: Greenhaven, 2010.

Dennis Love, *My City Was Gone: One American Town's Toxic Secret, Its Angry Band of Locals, and a $700 Million Day in Court*. New York: HarperPerennial, 2007.

David Michaels, *Doubt Is Their Product*. New York: Oxford University Press, 2009.

David Naguib Pellow, *Resisting Global Toxics: Transnational Movements for Environmental Justice*. Cambridge, MA: MIT Press, 2007.

Philip Shabecoff and Alice Shabecoff, *Poisoned Profits*. New York: Random House, 2008.

Mark E. Stelljes, *Toxicology for Nontoxicologists*. Lanham, MD: Scarecrow, 2008.

Web Sites

Agency for Toxic Substances and Disease Registry (www.atsdr.cdc. gov). A federal public health agency of the U.S. Department of Health and Human Services, ATSDR serves the public by providing trusted health information to prevent harmful exposures and diseases related to toxic substances. The site features a comprehensive alphabetical listing of toxic chemicals and their uses, history, and health effects.

Earth Portal (www.earthportal.org). The Earth Portal is a comprehensive Web site with timely, science-based information about the environment. The Earth Portal has three components: *The Encyclopedia* *of Earth*, with over 3,500 articles produced and reviewed by 1,000 scholars from 60 countries; the Earth Forum, which provides commentary from scholars and discussions with the general public; and Earth News, which offers news stories on environmental issues drawn from many sources.

The Hudson River Dredging Project (www.hudsondredging.com). This site, created by General Electric, follows the cleanup of the largest Superfund site in the United States. The Web site contains up-to-date information on the dredging, technical aspects, photos and videos of the cleanup efforts, press releases, and rebuttals to environmentalists.

The Neighborhood Toxicologist (http://theneighborhoodtoxicologist. blogspot.com). The neighborhood toxicologist summarizes information on chemical contaminants that impact peoples' daily lives and the environment. Several hundred informative articles written by independent toxicologist Emily Monosson cover dozens of toxic substances and their effects on human health and the environment.

Superfund365: A Site a Day (www.superfund365.org). Starting on September 1, 2007, Superfund365 visited one Superfund toxic waste site each day for a full year, starting in New York City and ending in Hawaii. Each site visited is featured in a Web page with photos, facts, history, cleanup costs, and information about the people who live near the site.

The Truth About Dow (www.thetruthaboutdow.org). Describing itself as the Dow Accountability Network, this organization monitors Dow Chemical Company's activities worldwide and takes stands against those activities. The Web site offers the group's perspectives on Dow's products as well as on the company's present and past business practices.

Source Notes

Overview

1. U.S. Senate Committee on Environment and Public Works, "Solid Waste Disposal Act," December 31, 2002. http://epw.senate.gov.
2. Olurominiyi Ibitayo, "Transboundary Dumping of Hazardous Waste," *The Encyclopedia of Earth*, August 26, 2008. www.eoearth.org.
3. Environmental Protection Agency, "Cradle-to-Grave Environmentally Compliant, No-VOC Furniture Coating," November 23, 2009. http://cfpub.epa.gov.
4. Quoted in Jeff Montgomery, "Miss. DuPont Plant Facing Lawsuits," Environmental Working Group, 2009. www.ewg.org.
5. Quoted in Elizabeth Grossman, *High Tech Trash*. Washington, DC: Island Press, 2006, p. 6.
6. Environmental Protection Agency, "Waste Minimization," May 6, 2009. www.epa.gov.

How Serious a Problem Is Toxic Waste?

7. Quoted in Charles Duhigg, "Clean Water Laws Are Neglected, at a Cost in Suffering," *New York Times*, September 12, 2009. www.nytimes.com.
8. Quoted in Duhigg, "Clean Water Laws Are Neglected, at a Cost in Suffering."
9. Quoted in Duhigg, "Clean Water Laws Are Neglected, at a Cost in Suffering."
10. Elizabeth M. Whelan, "Chemicals and Newborns: Womb Mates?" American Council on Science and Health, July 14, 2005, www.acsh.org.
11. Quoted in David Biello, "Are Some

Chemicals More Dangerous at Low Doses?" *Scientific American*, April 3, 2009. www.scientificamerican.com.

Are Toxic Waste Cleanup Efforts Working?

12. Quoted in Robin McKie, "Sellafield: The Most Hazardous Place in Europe," *Guardian*, April 19, 2009. www.guardian.co.uk.
13. Quoted in Joaquin Sapien and Richard Mullins, "Superfund Today," Center for Public Integrity, April 26, 2007. http://projects.publicintegrity.org.
14. David Gargill "The General Electric Superfraud," *Harpers*, December 2009, p. 43.
15. Environmental Protection Agency, "Record of Decision (ROD) & Responsiveness Summary," October 2, 2009. www.epa.gov.
16. Gargill, "The General Electric Superfraud," p. 46.

How Big a Threat Is Electronic Waste?

17. Quoted in *60 Minutes*, "Following the Trail Of Toxic E-Waste," August 30, 2009. www.cbsnews.com.
18. Quoted in *60 Minutes*, "Following the Trail Of Toxic E-Waste."
19. Chris Carroll, "High Tech Trash," *National Geographic*, January 2008. http://ngm.nationalgeographic.com.
20. Tom Zeller Jr., "Few Rules for Recycling Electronics," *New York Times*, May 31, 2009. www.nytimes.com.
21. Quoted in Mike Thomas, "H. Res. 938," Basel Action Network, November 19, 2009. www.ban.org.
22. Quoted in France 24, "Catastrophic

E-Waste Fuels Global Toxic Dump," November 13, 2009. www.france24. com.

23. Carroll, "High Tech Trash."
24. Quoted in Derrick Z. Jackson, "Electronics Dumping Ground," Basel Action Network, September 23, 2008. www.ban.org.
25. Quoted in Craig Kielburger and Marc Kielburger, "E-Waste Litters the Developing World," *Huffington Post*, May 12, 2008. www.huffingtonpost. com.
26. Quoted in Bharati Chaturvedi, "Dismantling India's E-Waste: Potential for Green Jobs?" *Huffington Post*, November 24, 2009. www.huffington post.com.
27. Quoted in Carroll, "High Tech Trash."
28. Carroll, "High Tech Trash."
29. Quoted in Matt Ford, "Sifting Through the Mounting Problem of E-

Waste," CNN, August 10, 2009. www. cnn.com.

What Is the Future of Toxic Waste?

30. Chaturvedi, "Dismantling India's E-Waste: Potential for Green Jobs?"
31. Chaturvedi, "Dismantling India's E-Waste: Potential for Green Jobs?"
32. Arnold Schwarzenegger, "Governor Schwarzenegger Signs Groundbreaking Legislation Implementing First-in-the-Nation Green Chemistry Program," Office of the Governor, September 29, 2008. http://gov.ca.gov.
33. Quoted in Ray Estrada, "California Sticks Toe in Green Chemistry Pond," Miller-McCune, July 27, 2009. www. miller-mccune.com.
34. Quoted in Estrada, "California Sticks Toe in Green Chemistry Pond."
35. Quoted in Estrada, "California Sticks Toe in Green Chemistry Pond."

List of Illustrations

Index

About the Author

Stuart A. Kallen is a prolific author who has written more than 250 non-fiction books for children and young adults over the past 20 years. His books have covered countless aspects of human history, culture, and science from the building of the pyramids to the music of the twenty-first century. Some of his recent titles include *How Should the World Respond to Global Warming? Romantic Art*, and *Communication with the Dead*. Kallen is also an accomplished singer-songwriter and guitarist in San Diego, California.